Exotic Tastes of
SRI LANKA

The Hippocrene Cookbook Library

Afghan Food & Cookery
African Cooking, Best of Regional
Albanian Cooking, Best of
Argentina Cooks!
Australia, Good Food From
Austrian Cuisine, Best of, Exp. Ed.
Belgian Cookbook, A
Brazilian Cookery, The Art of
Bulgarian Cooking, Traditional
Burma, Flavors of,
Cajun Women, Cooking With
Caucasus Mountains, Cuisines of the
Croatian Cooking, Best of, Exp. Ed.
Czech Cooking, Best of, Exp. Ed.
Danube, All Along The, Exp. Ed.
Dutch Cooking, Art of, Exp. Ed.
Egyptian Cooking
Eritrea, Taste of
Filipino Food, Fine
Finnish Cooking, Best of
French Caribbean Cuisine
French-English Dictionary of
   Gastronomic Terms
French Fashion, Cooking in the (Bilingual)
Greek Cuisine, The Best of, Exp. Ed.
Haiti, Taste of
Havana Cookbook, Old (Bilingual)
Hungarian Cookbook
Hungarian Cooking, Art of, Rev. Ed.
Icelandic Food & Cookery
Indian Spice Kitchen
International Dictionary of Gastronomy
Irish-Style, Feasting Galore
Italian Cuisine, Treasury of (Bilingual)
Japanese Home Cooking
Korean Cuisine, Best of
Laotian Cooking, Simple
Latvia, Taste of

Lithuanian Cooking, Art of
Mayan Cooking
Mongolian Cooking, Imperial
Norway, Tastes and Tales of
Persian Cooking, Art of
Poland's Gourmet Cuisine
Polish Cooking, Best of, Exp. Ed.
Polish Country Kitchen Cookbook
Polish Cuisine, Treasury of (Bilingual)
Polish Heritage Cookery, III. Ed.
Polish Traditions, Old
Portuguese Encounters, Cuisines of
Pyrenees, Tastes of
Quebec, Taste of
Rhine, All Along The
Romania, Taste of, Exp. Ed.
Russian Cooking, Best of, Exp. Ed.
Scandinavian Cooking, Best of
Scotland, Traditional Food From
Scottish-Irish Pub and Hearth Cookbook
Sephardic Israeli Cuisine
Sicilian Feasts
Slovak Cooking, Best of
Smorgasbord Cooking, Best of
South African Cookery, Traditional
South American Cookery, Art of
South Indian Cooking, Healthy
Spanish Family Cookbook, Rev. Ed.
Sri Lanka, Exotic Tastes of
Swiss Cookbook, The
Syria, Taste of
Taiwanese Cuisine, Best of
Thai Cuisine, Best of, Regional
Turkish Cuisine, Taste of
Ukrainian Cuisine, Best of, Exp. Ed.
Uzbek Cooking, Art of
Wales, Traditional Food From
Warsaw Cookbook, Old

Exotic Tastes of
SRI LANKA

Suharshini Seneviratne

HIPPOCRENE BOOKS
NEW YORK

Book and jacket design by Acme Klong Design, Inc.

For more information, address:
HIPPOCRENE BOOKS, INC.
171 Madison Avenue
New York, NY 10016

ISBN 0-7818-0966-5

Cataloging-in-Publication Data available from the Library of Congress.
Printed in the United States of America.

Contents

Introduction 3

The Sri Lankan Spice Rack 9

Glossary of Ingredients and Terminology 11

Utensils and Apparatuses 28

Measurements and Suggestions 31

Appetizers 33

Salads 53

Rice and Other Staples 73

Vegetables 97

Poultry, Eggs, and Meats 125

Seafood 149

Desserts 179

Sweetmeats 197

Authentic Meals 217

Mild Dishes 221

Index 222

Introduction

The breathtaking tropical island of Sri Lanka lies in the Indian Ocean, separated from southeastern India by a mere 30-mile chain of shoals. This physical proximity to India has inevitably influenced Sri Lankan cuisine, and today these ties are particularly evident in certain urad dhal-based northern Sri Lankan foods. However, over the centuries the majority of these recipes have been modified to suit the local palate.

The island covers an area of 25,332 square miles, extending 270 miles north to south and 140 miles east to west. The terrain of this tropical paradise varies dramatically from the tea-carpeted mountains and valleys of the south-central hill country through the coastal plains of luscious paddy fields, rubber plantations, and typical dry zones to golden sandy beaches. The mountains are home to the country's precious rain forests and give rise to its numerous rivers and cascading waterfalls. Formally known as Ceylon, Serendib, and Taprobane, today Sri Lanka is officially the Democratic Socialist Republic of Sri Lanka.

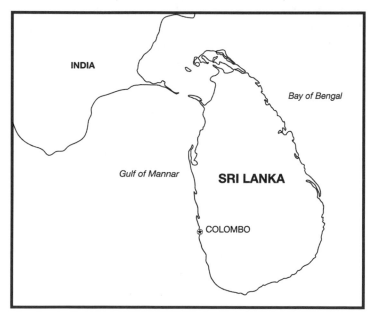

Historically, Sri Lanka's geographic location as an ideal trading post, along with its flourishing spice gardens, enticed Europeans to the island. The Portuguese, Dutch, and British in turn have greatly influenced the native cuisine and introduced innovative ingredients, recipes, and cooking techniques to its repertoire. The Portuguese occupied Sri Lanka from 1505 to 1658, followed by the Dutch from 1658 to 1796. The Dutch rule was enforced by the Dutch East India Company—a seventeenth century European government charter composed of several private commercial companies. The British undertook the

3

surrendered Dutch strongholds in 1802 and conquered the Kandyan kingdom in 1815. In 1948, Ceylon gained independence, thus opening the doors on an era of liberation, pride, and rejuvenation.

Before the European waves of colonization, 2,400 years of kings and kingdoms prevailed. Anuradhapura, the royal capital of the Sinhalese kingdom, flourished for over a thousand years, followed by an equally prosperous royal capital in Polonnaruwa. The Kandyan kingdom, the only kingdom that repelled conquests by the Portuguese and Dutch, was the last to fall. The ruins, treasures from antiquity, demonstrate the great vision and grandeur of the times as well as the skills and panache of the architects and artisans. Among them are beautiful Buddhist temples with monumental stupas; colossal granite Buddha statutes; multicomplexed monasteries; sprawling palaces with planned gardens; channel-guided water circulatory mechanisms for cooling; giant tanks; lakes and reservoirs; swimming pools; and baths.

The 20 million people of Sri Lanka are of diverse ethnicities—Sinhalese, Tamil, Muslim, Burgher, Malay, and Vedda—but are jointly renowned for their endearing smiles and warm hospitality. The Sinhaleses are Sri Lanka's majority population; they constitute 75 percent of its population, while the Tamils are the nation's principal minority. An extreme minority today, the Veddas are Sri Lanka's oldest people and an important aspect of the country's heritage. Sinhala is the primary language of the island, followed by Tamil and English. Often, based on region and ethnicity, different dialects are spoken and colorful accents are developed. Walking hand in hand with the multiple cultures are diverse religions and, in turn, a plethora of colorful customs and festivals that further enhance and enrich the local scene.

Sri Lanka has been a predominantly a Buddhist nation since it adopted the religion around the third century B.C. Buddhist temples with monumental dome-shaped relic chambers from both the past and present scatter the isle and are constant reminders of peace, tranquility, and humanity. *Poya*, observed monthly on the day of the full moon, is a national holiday marked for paying homage to Buddha and in furthering spiritual growth. Buddhist festivals in Sri Lanka are chiefly observed on a full-moon day. *Vesak* is a popular Buddhist festival to honor the birth, enlightenment, and passing of Buddha. Celebrated in May, this is a holy day for prayer and worship as well as a day of grand celebration. At dusk, the country gradually transforms as it comes alight with myriad twinkling lights, simple and elaborate multistructured intricate lanterns, and huge *pandals* (illuminated displays that depict scenes from the Buddha's life and previous lives). During this day of giving, refreshments are distributed to passersby from roadside stalls known as *dan sal*, while free meals are served to the needy. The large lanterns are often kept until *Posson*. Observed in June, it commemorates the advent of Buddhism to the Land. On this day pilgrims gather at the ancient site of Mihintale, where it is believed the first doctrine was preached. The annual *perehara* (procession) of the Temple of The Tooth

Relic in Kandy is a spectacular event. The highlight of this procession is the carrying of the ornate casket (containing the tooth relic of the Buddha) on a magnificent elephant highly adorned with glittering gold and precious gems.

The Sinhalese Tamil New Year dawns around April 13th on an auspicious hour favored by astrologers of repute. This traditional New Year is a time for togetherness, family, and friends. The celebrants prepare for this event days in advance by spring-cleaning and whitewashing their homes; flocking to stores for gifts and new clothes; and making traditional sweetmeats. The *Nonakathe*, or non-auspicious period, which could last up to a day, precedes the New Year. The New Year dawns at the auspicious hour to the deafening sounds of firecrackers and drums. Dressed in new clothes of a lucky color, one faces the auspicious direction and lights the stove. As a symbol of prosperity, milk is boiled in an open pot and allowed to overflow. Dressed in smart new clothes, families sit down to a table laden with traditional foods and sweetmeats, and the first bites of *kiri bath* (milk rice) are taken. For it marks a new beginning, this occasion is a customary time to seek forgiveness from those wronged. On this day and throughout the season, elders are revered, games are played, traditional songs are sung, relatives are visited (and gifts exchanged), and a host of other traditions and customs are observed.

Hinduism, a parasol religion under which many deities are revered, is the predominant religion of Sri Lankan Tamils. Depending on region and livelihood, the importance of the many deities may vary. Lord Shiva, Vishnu, Ganesh, and Skantha are revered, along with many others. The colorful Hindu festivals are numerous and followed in the style of southern India. In January, Hindu homes island-wide celebrate the harvest festival known as *Thai Pongal*. Many rites are observed on the day: A pot of milk is boiled over as a predictor of good fortune and intricate designs called *kolam* are drawn to decorate doorsteps and inner courtyards. Special foods and sweetmeats are made and *pongal*, a sweet preparation of rice, coconut milk, and jaggery, is a must on the occasion. *Deepavali*, the "festival of lights," symbolizes the victory of virtuousness and the elevating of spiritual darkness. Hindu homes are brightly lit with oil lamps and lights to welcome Lakshmi, goddess of wealth and fortune. In August, the Hindu community celebrates the chariot festival, *Vel*, where an intricately chiseled chariot adorned with assorted flowers carries a statue and weapons of the god Skantha. A white cow, the sacred animal of the Hindus and believed vehicle of the god, is adorned with colorful garlands and painted horns before drawing the chariot in a colorful procession down decorated streets.

Catholicism was introduced to Sri Lanka during the Portuguese occupation of the land. Saint's days are celebrated in flag-strung open squares before highly ostentatious church facades. Protestantism was introduced by the Dutch and encouraged by the British, which resulted in the country's significant Christian community. Christmas among other religious holidays, is celebrated in Sri Lanka with similar customs as in the rest of the Christian world.

Muslims believe in Islam and live a life based on the holy Koran, which relays the teachings of Islam. The predominant Muslim celebration observed by Sri Lankan Muslims is the *Id* or *Ramazan* celebration. The sighting and positioning of the moon determine the exact date of the celebration, which is always preceded by one month of fasting by Muslim devotees. *Ramazan*, a time of peace and harmony, is a day of grand feasting shared by family and friends. Mosques are attended, prayers are chanted, gifts are exchanged, and platters of food are offered to neighbors. The delicious *buriyani* rice and *wattalappam* pudding are a must on this occasion. Sri Lanka celebrates a host of other days and seasons of religious and cultural importance that are beyond the scope of this book.

As a nation of multiple cultures and faiths, the predominant groups of the island have been instrumental in enriching and developing the cuisine: Most likely, the Hindus and Buddhists played a pivotal role in refining the vegetarian dishes; the Christians the beef and pork recipes; and the Muslims the mutton and lamb preparations. Further, based on the region of origin, variations of a recipe have often been introduced to the repertoire. In particular, the northern, southern, and central regions of the country take great pride in their unique flavors and individuality. Sri Lankan cuisine has been held close to the heart, passed down to many generations, and evolved into a colorful, unique, and adventurous masterpiece.

Since the entrées revolve around the nation's favorite food, rice, the loosely coined term "rice and curry" best describes Sri Lankan cuisine. A unique array of other staples, such as hoppers, *godamba roti*, and *pittu*, adds diversity to the local cuisine. The tone of traditional Sri Lankan food is set at "hot and spicy," for we are a nation that revels in our capacity to savor the heat a preparation offers. However, conventionally hot and spicy entrées are not always served fiery hot. Our cuisine does offer a wide array of mild recipes, and a traditional meal is often planned to include one or more mild dishes to complement a spicy hot preparation. The heat of a dish is predominantly controlled by the amount of chili used, be it in the form of chili powder, chili flakes, whole dry red chilies, fresh chilies, and/or curry powders. Since the amount of heat an individual can handle is best judged by that person alone, the proportions of chili Sri Lankan recipes call for can often be adjusted to taste without compromising the integrity of the dish.

The gloriously aromatic and flavorful herbs and spices are renowned for their capacity to enhance the most humble foods. The lavish use of these ingredients in savory entrées, desserts, and side dishes is a popular practice in Sri Lankan cuisine. In our recipes, the spices are commonly used whole, ground, pan-roasted, or fried. Pan-roasting the spices encourages the release of their inherent oils. Whole spices are dry-roasted in a skillet that is gently shaken to prevent the spices from burning. Cardamom pods, cloves, cinnamon, coriander seeds, and fennel seeds are some of our favorite aromatic spices, while curry leaves, mint, lemongrass, and *rampa* or *pandan* are our most commonly used herbs. It is best to use fresh herbs, though the use of dry herbs is not unheard of.

Availability often dictates the choice ingredients of a cuisine. The most illustrious Sri Lankan ingredient is probably coconut, its unique flavor being the essence of our authentic island cuisine. Whether in a savory entrée or a sweet dessert, coconut contributes an enticing depth of flavor and texture to a dish. Its flavor is often introduced in traditional recipes in the form of freshly grated coconut, coconut milk, and/or coconut oil. In today's supermarkets, coconut is readily available in many innovative forms like desiccated coconut and coconut powder.

Sri Lankan cuisine is a relatively new flavor that is burgeoning in western cities like London, Toronto, New York, and Los Angeles. As with any other cuisine or art form, even a fundamental knowledge of Sri Lanka, its people, history, and culture will only add to the overall experience of its cuisine. With each delightful bite one will not only savor the unique and exotic tastes but also surrender to the heightened total experience.

The Sri Lankan Spice Rack

Combinations of the following ingredients are used to flavor authentic recipes and most often used in the indicated forms. The spices can be kept in airtight containers for months, while the fresh ingredients such as ginger and garlic are better kept refrigerated.

The recommended mail-order sites for Sri Lankan ingredients are www.slgrocer.com and www.srilankacurry.com

Black pepper: peppercorns, freshly milled
Cardamom: whole, ground to a powder
Cinnamon: sticks, ground to a powder
Cloves: whole, ground to a powder
Coriander: seeds, ground to a powder, fresh leaves
Cumin: seeds, ground to a powder
Curry leaves: whole
Dill: seeds, leaves
Fennel: seeds, leaves, ground to a powder
Fenugreek: seeds
Gamboge: cloves, ground to a paste
Garlic: cloves, powder, ground to a paste
Ginger: powder, ground to a paste
Green Chilies: whole
Jaffna Curry Powder
Lemongrass: stalk
Maldive Fish: flakes
Mustard: seeds, powder, ground to a paste
Rampa or Pandan: leaves
Raw Sinhala Curry Powder
Red chili: whole, dry whole, flakes, powder, flakes
Roasted Sinhala Curry Powder
Tamarind: pulp, paste
Turmeric: ground to a powder

Glossary of Ingredients and Terminology

The objective of this compilation is to inform the user on certain unfamiliar ingredients and cooking practices pertaining to Sri Lankan recipes.

ACHCHARU

The term refers to pickles in general. The *achcharu* can be simple, usually mixing pieces of an inherently sour fruit or raw fruit (mango, wood apple, etc.) with spicy seasonings such as chili, pepper, or mustard and salt. To balance the flavors it can be further seasoned with a touch of sugar. This version is best eaten within one to two hours. The more elaborate *achcharu* is cooked (parboiled or completely boiled) in vinegar and then mixed with spicy seasonings and sugar. This cooked version will keep well for a few weeks. The world of *achcharu* is vast but is fundamentally the same.

AMBUL-THIYAL

This fish or meat preparation is characterized by the use of gamboge, black pepper, and vinegar. The key ingredients result in a slightly tart dish that is usually moist to dry in consistency.

BADUM

A cooking technique where the ingredients are first stir-fried in oil and then simmered in coconut milk.

BUTTER CHILIES

This is a chili preparation commonly referred to as *moru miris*. The fresh chilies (usually spicy, fairly small, whole cayenne, Thai, arbol, etc.) are marinated in a mixture of buttermilk or yogurt and salt and dried over a few days. During the drying process, the chilies are basted with the marinade. The completely dried chilies can be stored successfully in an airtight container at room temperature. Butter chilies are served deep-fried (to a dark brown color) to introduce a punch and crunch to rice and curry meals.

CHILIES

The use of heat-inducing chilies is a popular practice in Sri Lankan cuisine. A wide array of chili types is grown and readily available today. In the western world, the words pepper and capsicum are used interchangeably with the word chili. Chilies are high in vitamin C and their heat covers a broad spectrum from mildly sweet to fiery hot. As a rule of thumb keep in mind that the smaller the chili the greater the heat. Further, the heat-inducing oils are contained in the seeds (attached inside the chili at the stem-end) and white veins or ribs (run along the length of the chili). Chilies are a very versatile ingredient used fresh, dried whole, dried ground, and dried crushed. Described below are chili varieties commonly used in Sri Lankan cuisine.

Arbol Chili: These fiery hot chilies measure about 3 inches in length and ¾ inch in width. These pointy brilliant red chilies have a glossy skin and are commonly dried and ground to make chili powder.

Capsicums: In Sri Lankan cuisine, the word is used to identify chilies that are approximately 7 inches long, 1½ to 2 inches wide (at the stem end), tapering to end in a slightly pointed tip, and light lime green (when tender). These chilies have a slightly waxy, glossy, and tough skin, and are commonly used for stuffing, in sautés, and as a vegetable. Capsicums have a slightly sweet bell pepper-like flavor with a variable heat. Similar varieties in the western market are Hungarian Wax, Anaheim (also known as California long green, hatch, and verde), and Cubanelle. Capsicums are used fresh and can be kept refrigerated for two to three weeks.

Green Chili: This refers to the unripe, vibrant green colored cayenne pepper. These chilies are slender, slightly wrinkled pods, green to red (depending on degree of ripeness) in hue, about ½ inch in width and 5 to 10 inches in length, and very spicy. (In Sri Lankan cuisine, a 4- to 5-inch-long chili is considered medium.) Used throughout Asia and definitely the most used chili in Sri Lankan cuisine, they are possibly the most popular chili variety cultivated worldwide. The fresh green chili is commonly used cut (sliced or slit lengthwise) and ground to a paste. The fresh ripe red pods are introduced to preparations as a ground paste or made into hot sauces, while the ripe dried pods are incorporated as whole (dried whole red), crushed (red chili flakes), and dried ground (chili powder). The dried forms keep well at room temperature stored in an airtight container. The green chilies keep at room temperature for one to two weeks (may ripen and change color) or refrigerated for two to three weeks, or frozen (in a freezer bag) for about two months.

Habañero Chili: Known in Sri Lanka as one of the *kochchi*, these lantern-shaped pods measure about 1½ inches long and 1½ inches wide (at the stem end). They are reputed to be the hottest of all chilies, so a little of it goes a long way. Their color varies from green, to yellow orange, to brilliant orange. The tender chilies with their inherent floral-fruity flavor and aroma are used in salads.

Thai Chili: In Asian cuisine a few varieties of chili are known as Thai chilies. In this instance, we are referring to the chili also known as bird's-eye. Approximately ¼ inch wide and 1½ inches long, these small, elongated, pointy green to red pods are fiery hot, and often presented with their stems intact. The fresh chilies can be used whole or ground, while the dried is used whole, crushed, or ground.

COCONUT

Coconut is the fruit of the tall, graceful coconut palm tree and grows in bunches of eight to twelve. The coconut as we know it is the seed of the fruit and it is encased in a highly fibrous husk (green when tender and tan when mature). The husked mature coconut has a round shape and a tough, fibrous, brown shell. The top (stem end) of the coconut has three small round, dark, indented markings called eyes. Beneath the shell is a layer of the white meat that when tender is soft and jelly-like and firms up as the fruit matures. This mature meat is what is commonly used in recipes. It surrounds a pool of mildly sweet liquid called coconut water (also referred to as coconut milk and not to be confused with the coconut milk extract used in recipes). When choosing a coconut, a less mature fruit will be heavy for its size and when shaken barely make any sound, while the more mature fruit (having less moist meat) will be light for its size and when shaken make more sound. For the recipes in this book, an average coconut is best. To open the coconut, soak it in water for 30 to 50 minutes. Then hold the coconut in one hand over the kitchen sink (if not using the coconut water, which can be drunk or incorporated into certain foods), and tap the shell hard with a large heavy blunt edged knife. Rotate the coconut so that the shell is cracked open crosswise in two halves. Pieces can be carefully cut or, more commonly, a coconut scraper is used to grate the coconut. Whether in a savory entrée or sweet dessert, coconut contributes an enticing depth of flavor and texture to a recipe. The flavor of coconut is often introduced in recipes in the form of freshly grated coconut, coconut milk, and/or coconut oil. In authentic dishes, coconut milk is used in two forms: The first extract is the default for the recipes in this book and is generally thicker and creamier than the second extract. Essentially, mixing freshly grated coconut with boiling water (1:1 ratio), straining and extracting the milk yields the first extract, while the second extract is obtained by repeating this process with the coconut left over from the first extraction. Whole coconuts are available in most supermarkets and more readily in Asian and Hispanic grocery stores. The un-cracked coconut will keep for one to two weeks at cool room temperature. Grated fresh coconut will keep for about one week refrigerated and about three months frozen, while the coconut milk once extracted can be refrigerated for about three days.

The following are innovative forms of coconut that are readily available.

Canned Coconut Milk: The canned milk is a rich, thick extract that can be used as is or mixed with either water or milk and then added to a curry or soup. Shake the can well and make sure the contents are evenly blended before use. The unopened can keeps well at room temperature. Once opened, transfer to an airtight container and the milk will keep for three to four days in the refrigerator and for about a month in the freezer.

Coconut Milk Powder: Sealed airtight packages of coconut milk powder are available in Asian, Oriental, and Hispanic grocery stores. It makes an ideal substitute for coconut milk and is used in the preparation of curries, soups, and desserts. To use, add it to warm or hot water (or milk) and mix until thoroughly blended. Depending on the amount of powder used and if water or milk is used, a rich first extract or a thin second extract can be mimicked. It could also be added straight to a cooking preparation and stirred well. The unopened package keeps well at room temperature, and once opened it will keep for three to four months in an airtight container at room temperature.

Desiccated Coconut: Desiccated coconut is the dehydrated form of grated or shredded fresh coconut. It has a long shelf life (about four months at room temperature, five to six months refrigerated, and eight to twelve months frozen. Desiccated coconut can be used as is in certain recipes or rehydrated with warm water (preferably) when substituted for grated coconut. Used in both savory and sweet preparations (when substituting), it is highly preferred over shredded coconut (a desiccated coconut with fairly large shavings). Sweetened desiccated coconut (flakes and shredded) is also available; it is good in certain cakes and sweets but rarely used in Sri Lankan cuisine.

Frozen Coconut Cream: This version is highly rich, with an intense coconut flavor and a beautiful creamy smooth texture. Thaw before using. When subjecting to heat (soups, curries, etc.) it is best added at the last minute as coconut cream has a very high tendency to split. It freezes well.

CURRY POWDERS

Curry powders are mélanges of specific spices mixed to exact proportions. They can be either purchased or made at home. Three curry powders are commonly used in Sri Lankan recipes: Jaffna Curry Powder, Raw Sinhala Curry Powder, and Roasted Sinhala Curry Powder. Curry powders will keep for months when stored in airtight containers. The recipes below divulge the secrets to these unique powders. To control their heat in you can slightly alter the amount of chili and pepper and counter-alter the amount of coriander.

Jaffna Curry Powder: This curry powder appears orange-brown in color and is used to flavor meat, seafood, and vegetarian recipes.

Pan-roast on low heat separately and then grind to a powder 1 pound whole dry red chilies, 1½ to 1¾ pounds coriander seeds, 4½ ounces fennel seeds, 2½ to 2¾ ounces cumin seeds, ¼ to ½ ounce black peppercorns, 4½ ounces curry leaves (leave a few whole), and ½ ounce turmeric powder. Combine all the spices.

Raw Sinhala Curry Powder: This curry powder is raw-green in color and is best used in vegetable preparations. It is sometimes marketed as Roasted Curry Powder.

Grind to a powder 9 ounces coriander seeds, 4½ ounces cumin seeds, 4½ ounces fennel seeds, 30 curry leaves, 10 cloves, 10 cardamom pods, and a 2-inch stick of cinnamon. Combine all the spices.

Roasted Sinhala Curry Powder: This curry powder is dark in color and a popular additive to traditional meat recipes. It is also used with certain seafood preparations. Since it is highly concentrated in flavor, a little goes a long way. It is commonly used together with turmeric powder and black pepper. (It is also sold as Dark Roasted Curry Powder and Sri Lankan Curry Powder.)

Pan-roast on low heat separately and then grind to a powder 1 pound whole dry red chilies, 9 ounces coriander seeds, 4½ ounces cumin seeds, 4½ ounces fennel seeds, 20 curry leaves (leave a few whole), 10 cloves, 10 cardamom pods, and a 2-inch stick of cinnamon. Combine all the spices.

FISH

A popular item in Sri Lankan cuisine, its preparation has been mastered to an art. Fish is a highly perishable ingredient, thus best used as fresh as possible. You should preferably store the cleaned, gutted, and cut (your fishmonger will do this for you) fish in the freezer. It is best to purchase the fish from a wharf. Look for firm, undamaged flesh that does not smell fishy but rather smells like fresh seawater. The surface of the fish should be clear and almost translucent, with no spots or patches of color indicative of bruising, spoilage, and freezer burn. When buying whole fish, look for clear bright eyes, red gills, intact scales, and shiny skin. Frozen fish should not look dry and/or have brown patches, as these are definite signs of freezer burn.

Fish cooks within a few minutes, so it is best to avoid overcooking the delicate fish. Larger whole fish are typically baked or grilled, while the small ones are good candidates for deep-frying and currying. Fish are either cut across the length into steaks (the larger steaks could be cut into fillets) or along the length into fillets. The following are popular in Sri Lankan cuisine:

Anchovy: Also referred to as sprat, this soft, delicate small bony fish have a distinct intense flavor. Fresh anchovies are delicious batter-fried and also good for *ambul-thiyal*. Canned anchovies (packed in salt or oil) are used to flavor other foods (salads, pizza, etc.). Dried anchovies (*karavala*), a popular food in Sri Lankan cuisine, can be sautéed, deep-fried (and added to foods), and curried. Smelts can be substituted for anchovy.

Jack Mackerel: Also known as mackerel, this fish has a mild to strong fishy flavor and a blue gray color. It grows to about 12 inches in length and has a high fat content. It is at its best when grilled, baked, or steamed. The readily available canned fish is commonly used to make fillings for appetizers.

Kingfish: Commonly referred to as seer, this fish is also called king mackerel. Kingfish measures 3½ to 4 feet in length and about 8 inches in width at its largest. The delicate white flesh has a mild yet distinct flavor and a moderately soft texture. A versatile fish, it is good for currying, sautéing, grilling, baking, frying, pickling, and drying (and made into *karavala*).

Sardine: Commonly referred to as *hurulla*, this fish is best deep-fried country-style. It can also be prepared in a curry, broiled, or roasted. Sardines have a moderately soft texture and a full flavor. When fresh it could easily be mistaken for herring, which is no crime as it is an ideal substitute for sardine.

Shark: The flesh of this fish is pinkish to ivory in color, highly meaty, and mild in flavor. It makes a good substitute for swordfish.

Spanish Mackerel: This versatile fish grows to about 12 inches in length. Its skin has characteristic spots, while its texture and flavor put him between jack mackerel and kingfish. It is good for currying, grilling, baking, etc.

Swordfish: This fish has a tough skin and its meaty flesh is off-white in color and rich in flavor. This versatile fish is great for grilling, sautéing, and for *ambul-thiyal*.

Tuna: The flesh of this firm-textured, bold and intensely flavored fish is pale pink to deep red in color. It is used in the preparation of maldive fish, a key ingredient in Sri Lankan cuisine. Tuna is good grilled and great prepared as *ambul-thiyal*.

GAMBOGE

In Sri Lankan households, this is better known as *goraka*. A fleshy fruit of a tropical shady tree, it is harvested when ripe (usually a deep yellow or orange hue), separated into cloves, and either sun-dried or dried in a furnace. When dry, the cloves look wrinkled and take on a deep, almost black, hue. *Goraka* is rich in vitamin C, has a unique sour flavor, and is used in Sri Lankan cuisine to both flavor and preserve foods. Dry *goraka* can be kept as is or mixed with vinegar and rock salt, which softens the cloves and makes them easier to grind. *Goraka* can be substituted with ripe tamarind except when it is a signature ingredient of a preparation (as in *ambul-thiyal*).

GHEE
Cooked longer than clarified butter, ghee is the purest form of butter. As a result of the longer cooking time in its production, the sugars slightly caramelize to impart a beautiful nutty flavor. Popular among vegetarians, vegetable ghee is made from vegetable oils that are clarified and made solid via hydrogenation. As a highly refined butter, it has a high burning point and hence is good for deep-frying. Ghee is used to flavor rice preparations, flat breads, and sweets.

JAGGERY
Jaggery, also known as palm sugar, is an exotic sweetener often used in Sri Lankan sweetmeats. *Kithul* jaggery is derived from the *kithul* palm (from the sap released when the large *kithul* flower is cut) and often used in traditional recipes. The quality of jaggery can vary from the purest rich, dark, and soft (easily broken with the hand) one to low quality, lighter colored, hard (some are rock hard), mixed with sugar versions. The sweetness of jaggery is best described to be between rich treacle and dark brown sugar and often when a recipe calls for jaggery the rich *kithul* jaggery is implied. To substitute would compromise the flavor and the integrity of the recipe. Jaggery is best stored at room temperature, wrapped in the dry plantain leaf it was presented in, and placed in an airtight container.

KALU POL
Literally translated, it means "black coconut" and is a special preparation of coconut that is added to a dish. *Kalu pol* has a unique rich flavor and texture. It is a concoction of coconut, whole dry chili, garlic, ginger, rice and mustard seeds that is pan-roasted until dark brown (almost black), mixed with a little water, and ground to a smooth paste. This is usually prepared immediately before use.

KARAVALA
Karavala, or dry fish, is a popular item in Sri Lankan cuisine. Both large (gutted, and stripped down the middle lengthwise) and small (whole) fish and even prawns are salted and sun-dried to produce this unique food. Dry fish is today available at most Asian and Oriental grocery stores. Wrapped in a paper bag or newspaper and contained in an airtight container, it will keep for about

six months in the refrigerator. The more dehydrated and salted the fish is the longer it will keep. Before using it, wash the dry fish thoroughly, as it could contain sand residues from being dried on sandy beaches.

KITHUL TREACLE

This is a beautiful, dark golden brown rich syrup derived from the *kithul* palm (from the sap released when the large *kithul* flower is cut). This treacle has a unique rounded sweetness that gives many traditional sweetmeats their distinct flavor. The unopened bottle or tin can be stored for many months at room temperature, while the opened one will keep for about a month when refrigerated.

LENTILS

Commonly known as dhal, numerous varieties are cultivated. A dhal usually is the husked, split form of the grain. The most popular dhal in Sri Lankan cuisine are misoor, moong, urad, and chana. Lentils are rich in proteins (an ideal source of protein for vegetarians) and are good curried, either on their own or mixed with vegetables, meats, or rice. Lentils can be stored for months in an airtight container. Soaking before cooking considerably reduces the cooking times of lentils.

Chana: This yellow, slightly larger dhal, is delicious curried, soaked and deep-fried, pureed and made into *vadai*. Chana flour, also known as *ata* flour, is a popular ingredient in Indian cuisine.

Misoor: The most popular dhal in Sri Lankan cuisine, it is also called red lentils. This dhal is a rich orange hue, does not require soaking before cooking, and cooks to a soft texture and taste and a yellow hue. It is also good cooked with spinach, and pureed and made into *vadai*.

Moong: The unhusked whole grain is dusty green color, while the husked is a pale yellow. It is available both whole and split. Husked moong dhal is ground to a cream-colored flour and is used in the preparation of traditional sweetmeats. The whole lentils are soaked and boiled (to a starchy, fluffy texture and a grayish color). They are good served with grated fresh coconut and *lunu miris* or *katta sambol*. The dhal can be pan-roasted (to reduce cooking time) for about 10 minutes and curried.

Urad: The un-husked grain is dark greenish black in color while the husked is a pale cream color. The dhal is soaked, pureed and used to prepare staples like *thosai* and *idly*. The husked split grains are also good curried.

MALDIVE FISH

A popular ingredient in Sinhalese recipes, maldive fish is commonly referred to as *umbalakada*. Large fillets of tuna are blanched in boiling water, tightly twisted and either sun-dried or furnace-dried to result in what we call maldive fish. This relatively expensive ingredient has a solid consistency and is prepared for use by either pounding into or chiseling out small pieces or flakes. The addition of maldive fish when called for by a recipe often gives the food its authentic Sri Lankan flavor.

MALLUM

This is a cooked vegetable and coconut-infused salad, traditionally served warm. *Vara* is probably the sole exception, as it is in effect a fish *mallum*. *Mallum* could also be considered a side dish and even as an entrée.

MARMITE

Available in bottled form, marmite is a thick, dark almost black, and smooth paste-like spread. This highly flavorful yeast extract is completely vegetable-based. It is a highly rich natural source of vitamin B and a good source of folic acid. It is equally flavorful spread over bread and butter, mixed with hot water and made into a warm nutritious drink, or used in foods such as soups, stews, etc. Tightly capped, it will keep for months at room temperature. Vegemite (a different brand based on the same principles) makes a good substitute for marmite.

PANI POL

The literal translation reads "honey coconut." *Pani pol* is a beautiful sweet, rich blend of coconut, treacle (or jaggery), and one or more aromatic spices (cinnamon, clove, cardamom, or nutmeg) that is delicately cooked to perfection. It is used in the preparation of traditional sweetmeats and desserts.

PAPPADAM

Pappadam are delicate paper-thin rounds of dried pastry that are either potato- (the most popular in Sri Lankan cuisine), rice-, and/or urad dhal-based. They are of varying sizes and could be plain or flavored (usually the rice variety) with cumin, fennel, or coarse black pepper. In their dried state, *pappadam* will keep for months in an airtight container. They are deep-fried (they swell out when fried) before serving. Rice and/or urad dhal *pappadam* are usually cooked over an open flame or on a hot cast-iron pan. *Pappadam* are an ideal accompaniment to rice and curry meals.

PILAU

This is a rice preparation where the rice first is delicately sautéed in butter or oil with aromatic ingredients and then simmered in water or stock. This gives the dish a beautiful nutty flavor and fragrance. Pilaus vary from simple to elaborate.

RICE

A multitude of rice varieties are cultivated worldwide. Because rice is cultivated in Sri Lanka and considered a staple, our cuisine sees the introduction of numerous rice varieties to its repertoire.

Rice color is determined by the presence or absence of the bran and germ. If attached, it is a brown rice, red rice, or black rice, and if removed, it is white rice.

Unlike white rice, the colored rice is highly nutritious, rich in vitamins (especially vitamin B), minerals, and fiber but on the down side also requires a longer cooking time. The length of the rice grain (white or colored) is a good indicator of its cooked consistency. The rice varies from long- to medium- to short-grain types. Long-grain rice is three to five times its width and when cooked has a light and fluffy consistency where the grains separate easily. Less than twice their width, the medium and short-grain varieties when cooked usually yields a thicker preparation and the grains tend to stick together. There are always exceptions to the rule. Aromatic types of rice are popular today and favored for their nutty or floral aromas. Further, as expected, the higher the quality of the grain the pricier it would be. Sri Lankan cuisine is not very picky or exacting as to the type of rice used, especially for the steamed version served daily, but high quality rice is preferred for the special rice preparations. The following are popular rice types for special and daily Sri Lankan rice preparations.

Basmati: This beautifully perfumed long-grained rice (white or brown) fluffs to perfection when cooked. The white variety is commonly used in special preparations like *buriyani*, tamarind rice, and rice pilau.

Jasmine Rice: This long-grain aromatic white rice resembles medium-grain rice. Popular in oriental cuisine, jasmine rice has been incorporated into the Sri Lankan repertoire. It cooks moist and tender and differs from the regular long-grain types in that it is denser and quite sticky. Its inherent coherent quality is preferred by some as the curries mixes well with the rice to give a perfect bite. It can be served daily (especially for lunch).

Red Country Rice: This nutritious pink to red (depending on the degree of bran and germ removal) rice has a distinct flavor that complements a variety of traditional dishes. It is highly perishable and is best kept refrigerated. Red rice requires a slightly longer cooking time than white rice. This rice is finely ground to make red rice flour.

Samba Rices: Three types are commonly known to Sri Lankans. *Sooduru samba* is a lovely medium-grain white rice and its elongated shape is similar to a cumin seed. This high-quality rice does not cohere when cooked and requires $1/4$ to $1/2$ cup less water to cook than long-grain rice. For elaborate rice preparations, this rice makes a perfect substitute for basmati rice. *Muthu samba* is a medium-grain rice that is oval and pearl-like and does not cohere when cooked. This high quality rice is favored in the preparation of yellow rice and fragrant fried rice. *Samba* is an in-between rice that is more common served plain (steamed or cooked in water) as a daily staple.

SAGO

A starch derived from the sago palm and a few other tropical palms is ground into flour and formed into tiny white pearl-like beads. The quick-cooking sago that is prevalent in today's supermarkets is a precooked form that requires no soaking before cooking. Sago is cooked in liquid, usually water and/or coconut milk, and made into a porridge or pudding. This dessert is commonly sweetened with jaggery, sugar, or treacle and is delicious served on its own or with fruit. This is a popular food in Asian and Oriental cuisines. When cooked, sago beads turn from opaque to translucent and the preparation thickens. Keep in mind that at a given cooking time the liquid may still be runny but once off the heat will still continue cooking and thickening. Sago can be stored in an airtight container for about three months.

SPICES AND HERBS

Cardamom: This popular spice is often used simultaneously with cloves. Made up of the dried pericarps of its flower, a cardamom pod is $2/5$ to $4/5$ inch long, oval-shaped, green (pale green when dried), and is used in its dried form. Each pod contains about twelve tiny, highly flavorful (fresh, sweet) and aromatic (strong, spicy), dark brown colored seeds. Cardamom is often used whole (pod) in rice preparations and ground (seeds) in desserts and sweetmeats. The aroma of freshly ground cardamom is subtle and comprises traces of ginger, coriander, nutmeg, and white pepper. Cardamom pods are best kept in their pericarps and only separated immediately before using.

Coriander: Coriander seeds (about $1/7$ inch, round, light brown) are used in their ground form to flavor traditional recipes and are a key ingredient in Sri Lankan curry powders. The flavor of this esteemed ingredient is best described as a beautiful bouquet of cardamom, cloves, white pepper, and orange. Coriander leaves are also known as cilantro. They resemble flat leaf parsley and have an acute bold flavor. Its flavor is perceived as a blend of parsley, juniper berries, mint, and spicy basil. Cilantro must be used fresh, for it does not preserve its flavor when dried.

Curry Leaves: Considered an herb, curry leaves are vibrant green, have a typical leaf shape with an uneven edge, and grow to approximately 3 inches in length. The "leaves," which have a prominent central vein, are truly leaflets that attach to a sprig. When crushed or fried in oil, they release a sweet and distinct fragrance. Curry leaves are commonly used to enhance the flavors of authentic entrées. Packed in an airtight container, they freeze beautifully. It is best to leave the sprigs intact before use. These leaves loose their integrity when dried.

Fenugreek: These seeds are small, light brown in color, and resemble tiny uneven stones. They have a bitter flavor until cooked. It is a commonly used ingredient in certain vegetable preparations, especially in the white curries.

Lemongrass: So named for its fragrance and appearance, this herb imparts a subtle refreshing lemon aroma and flavor to dishes. The approximately 2-feet-long gray-green stalks resemble grasses, but are more scallion-like. It is highly fibrous and only the 6 to 8-inch base is used after the top is cut off and a layer of tough outer leaves is peeled off.

Mustard: Brown mustard seeds are used in Sri Lankan cuisine. They are relatively smaller than their yellow or white counterparts. Brown mustard has a hot and slightly bitter flavor and is commonly used whole, ground into a powder, or ground with vinegar and a pinch of rock salt into a paste. The whole seeds are best used slightly toasted in a little oil until their aroma is released.

Pandan: In Sri Lankan households, this Asian herb is more commonly known as *rampa*. The pandan leaf is vibrant green and measures approximately 1½ to 2 inches in width, with a prominent vein running down the length of it. It can grow to about a foot in length. Small pieces of the leaf (fresh or dry) are commonly used in meat recipes and are certainly no strangers to vegetarian preparations. Certain recipes for Roasted Sinhala Curry Powder also incorporate a few pieces of pandan leaf.

Paprika: This is a spice comprising finely ground dried ripe chilies. The heat of paprika is never hot and ranges from bland to intense but mild, depending on the chili used. Sweet paprika is made from particularly sweet flavored chilies and carries no heat, as all or most of the seeds and veins are removed before its preparation. Conversely, hot paprika is made using hot chilies and some of the seeds and veins. The color of the paprika also varies from light orange to intense red depending on the chili used. For a milder version of the dishes in this book, paprika is the recommended substitute for chili powder. Avoid using the sweet paprika as it could alter the overall flavor of the recipe.

Saffron: The rich golden red stigmas hold tremendous fragrance and flavor as well as a golden hue.

When purchasing saffron consider that the deeper the color of the stigmas the higher its quality. When using saffron strands, they first are infused with a hot (not boiling) liquid, allowed time to color, and then the liquid is used. This process allows for the even flavoring and coloring of a recipe. Ground saffron is also used, but the pure form can be harder to distinguish from the adulterated versions.

Turmeric: The rhizome is utilized after having been dried and then ground to a deep yellow powder. This gorgeous spice tastes warm, musky, and gingery and a little goes a long way. The overuse of turmeric powder in a recipe can be extremely overpowering. It is used as a coloring and is often used as a substitute for saffron.

STEAMED FLOURS AND SEMOLINA

Traditional staples such as *pittu*, stringhoppers, *idly*, and certain sweetmeats require the steaming of one or more ingredient. All-purpose flour, rice flour (red or white), and semolina are often utilized steamed. This can be done in bulk, ahead of time, and stored in an airtight container. First, place the ingredient on a black and white newspaper or a few layers of muslin and wrap securely in a tight parcel. Place in a steamer and steam (the all-purpose flour for 45 to 50 minutes, rice flour for 25 to 30 minutes, and semolina for 20 to 25 minutes), replenishing the water as necessary with hot water. Take off the heat, unwrap, let cool a little, press down and break (as it may clump together) with hand or back of spoon, and sift. Cool to room temperature before using in a recipe. Ready to use (steamed or roasted) rice flour can be purchased.

TAMARIND

This is the rich, dark almost black pulp of the ripe tamarind seedpods. It has a deep tangy flavor when incorporated that gives preparations its distinct flavor. Commonly used in Indian cuisine, it is best when made into chutney and added to flavor fish recipes. When in season the ripe pods are occasionally available at Asian grocers. The packaged pulp (seedless) and containers of the paste (without seeds and fibers) are readily available. When choosing tamarind pulp look for dark, soft packages (avoid the dry ones) and when using mix well with warm water, strain out the fibers (and seeds, if from the whole pod) and extract all the wonderful flavor. Leftover pulp will keep for about three months stored in an airtight container.

TAPIOCA

See Cassava Root

THELDALA

This is a popular cooking technique where the ingredients are stir-fried and simmered in oil. When following this technique, it is best to add the chili towards the end of the cooking time (unless otherwise stated), as the chili tends to burn during cooking.

SUGAR CANDY

Commonly referred as *sookiri* in Sri Lankan cuisine, sugar candy is a sweetener with a unique mellow subtle flavor. It resembles small crystal-like, opaque rocks and comes in white and light brown forms. As a cooking ingredient (usually coarsely ground and used in sweetmeats), white sugar candy is the more popular while the brown (which contains caramelized sugar) is incorporated in home remedies for flu and soar throat.

VEGETABLES AND FRUITS

Ash Plantain: A plant and fruit similar to that of bananas, ash plantain is considered a vegetable and is green to yellow to brown-black in color depending on the stage of ripeness. In supermarkets, it is more frequently sold as cooking banana or plantain. The green fruit is used, which when cooked results in a subtle gray color (hence its name). In its green stage the starchy flesh yield a fluffy texture when cooked and is prepared in a curry, mashed like a potato, and is also delicious deep-fried. To deep-fry, peel the skin, cut into thin slices, and season with salt, lime juice, and chili powder. Ripe ash plantains have a sweet taste (as the starch turns to sugars) and are best either baked in their skin or sliced and deep-fried. As with the rest of the banana family this vegetable when uncooked has a tendency to discolor when exposed to air. The plantain flower bud is edible when cooked.

Breadfruit: The seasonal fruit of a large tropical tree, breadfruit is considered a vegetable. It has a round shape and is about the size of a cantaloupe. Its slightly thick skin is green when tender or mature and brownish yellow when ripe. It is covered with eyes that are very prominent in the mature fruit. The inedible stem and core must be removed either before or after cooking. The mature breadfruit is excellent cooked in a curry with creamy coconut milk and delicate spices. All stages of the fruit can be finely sliced and deep-fried. The tender and mature is usually used in savory dishes, hence it is seasoned with salt and chili powder, while for a sweet treat all stages (including the ripe) are seasoned with powdered sugar or sugar syrup. This versatile ingredient can also be steamed, boiled, baked, or roasted. If the green texture is preferred, cook the fruit immediately as it will ripen rapidly at room temperature. When ripe it is highly perishable and will keep two to three days in the refrigerator. Finely cut breadfruit can be blanched and sun-dried until totally dehydrated and kept for months in an airtight container. This version is then rehydrated and used to make mallum. Boiled tender or mature breadfruit is a popular food in Sri Lanka and is usually served with grated fresh coconut and *lunu miris* or *katta sambol*.

Cassava Root: The roots of cassava, a tropical plant, are edible when cooked. The cassava root has a tough brown skin, is elongated and fairly plump, yam-like, and firm. When cut, the flesh is white to cream. The root is cut, peeled, and cooked (best boiled, curried, and fried as chips). The cooked root is pale yellow with a light and fluffy texture. Traditionally, Sri Lankans serve the boiled cassava root with grated fresh coconut and *lunu miris* or *katta sambol*. It is also good with a spicy fish or meat curry. Tapioca is derived from the root of the cassava plant. Quick-cooking tapioca is prevalent in today's supermarkets; it is the precooked form that requires no soaking before cooking. These pear-like white beads resemble, cook, and keep like sago (see *Sago*).

Drumstick: This fruit of a tall dry-zone tree drumstick is also referred to as *murunga* in Sri Lankan cuisine. These drumstick-like fruits are 1 to 1^1/$_2$-feet in length and about ^{3}/$_4$-inch in width. They have an inedible fibrous skin, and when cooked their flesh is soft and delicate. The tender sticks are preferred for their flavor. Drumstick is best cut into about 3-inch lengths and cooked in a mild curry. To eat, the stick is opened up, put in the mouth (flesh side down), and pulled out. The flesh is scraped into the mouth with the front teeth and when eating it is simplest to use the hand. The approximately ^{1}/$_2$-inch oblong seeds are edible when cooked. Drumstick leaves are used to flavor the traditional Sri Lankan crab curry.

Gotukola: Both the leaves and tender stalks of this runner plant are edible. Rich in iron, *gotukola* must be used fresh and it makes a gorgeous salad and nutritious porridge. It can be substituted with parsley.

Jackfruit: The fruit of a large tropical tree, when tender and mature it is considered a vegetable and when ripe, a fruit. In Sri Lankan cuisine the tender, mature, and ripe are referred to as *polos*, *kos*, and *varaka* respectively. The tender fruit is about the size of a cantaloupe, is green and firm, and has a prickly, fairly thick skin. It is great as both a spicy curry and tangy pickle. The mature fruit is similar in size and shape to an extra-large watermelon. It is firm to the touch and has a thick, spiky, green skin. When cut, numerous 4-inch, firm, ivory color, elongated fruits (each has a seed inside) are attached to the thick core. They are called *madhulu*, and are compactly packaged and held by slightly stretchy ivory bands. These individual fruits are cleaned, cut, and either curried or boiled. When whole they are slit, seeded, stuffed and cooked. The seeds too are edible (excluding the outer shells) when cooked (used fresh or sun-dried). The ripe jackfruit emits a distinct fruity aroma and has a thick, spiky, greenish yellow color and a tender skin. The tender jackfruit will keep for about two days at room temperature and refrigerated for slightly longer while the mature fruits will keep parboiled for two to three days and the ripe fruits for about one week refrigerated.

Karavila: This vegetable is better known as bitter gourd, named so for its inherent bitter flavor. Measuring 4 to 8 inches in length, these elongated, pale green to rich green, wrinkled gourds hang from a creeper that extends via tendrils. For cooking, the tender and mature gourds are preferred over the ripe. Best sliced and deep-fried (can be incorporated into a salad) or cut into pieces and curried, they are also good pickled. The cooked seeds are edible. The hybrid variety is light green and less wrinkly, thicker and longer, and has a less bitter flavor. The unripe *karavila* can be refrigerated for three to four days.

Kathurumurunga: This medium size tree bears no relation to the drumstick (*murunga*) tree. The dark green leaflets of this exotic plant are edible and best sautéed (*theldala*) or made into a *mallum*. The cream white buds and flowers are especially delicious when sautéed and incorporated in omelets.

Long Beans: This very narrow (about 1/4 inch), long (1 to 1 3/4 feet), light green to green-brown pod is a fruit of a creeper plant. Because of their length and width, the pods tend to be slightly curled. Commonly referred to as *makaral* and *pythanga* in Sri Lankan cuisine, longbeans are also a popular ingredient in Thai cuisine. They are best cut into 1 to 1 1/2-inch pieces and sautéed or deep-fried and curried. The cut pieces can be frozen for two to three weeks.

Lotus Root: It is the crunchy, plump, and 5 to 8-inch rhizome of the lotus plant that is loosely termed root. The root has air holes that when sliced crosswise result in beautiful lace-like cut out flowers. When purchasing it, look for unblemished, beige roots without soft spots. Since the flesh has a high tendency to darken and discolor when exposed to air, once the skin is pared and the root sliced transfer to a bowl of water seasoned with vinegar or lime juice. A popular ingredient in oriental cuisines, lotus root is good sautéed, curried (in a *badum*) deep-fried, steamed, and braised. It will keep in the refrigerator for about four days.

Okra: Commonly called "ladies' fingers" in Southern Asia, these slender green pods are the young seedpods of a beautiful plant. Whole okra is delicious simply steamed or sautéed, while when cut they can be effectively sautéed, deep-fried, or curried. When choosing okra it is best to select the unblemished, tender, plump, and crisp pods. The mature pods are very fibrous and less flavorful. Okra is known to be sticky and slimy when cut (more so with the tender pod) but can be cooked with acid (tomatoes, lime, vinegar, etc.) to tone it to an enjoyable level. The tender okra seeds and flowers are edible too.

Wood Apple: Also referred to in Sri Lankan cuisine as *divul*, wood apples are the fruits of a large dry-zone tree. This exotic fruits are on average slightly larger than a tennis ball and have a tough, cream-beige, outer shell that must be cracked to get to its highly flavorful pulp. The pulp is amidst a mass of fibers; when raw it is pale green and has a sour flavor and when ripe it is a dark brown, almost black color. To prepare wood apple the pulp is scooped out (to leave an empty shell), dissolved in water, and strained. The extract is then sweetened and mixed with coconut milk to make a unique Sri Lankan dessert. The ripe flesh can also be made into jam. The ripe fruit keeps for about one week at room temperature and about two weeks refrigerated.

Utensils and Apparatuses

Sri Lankan cuisine requires some basic utensils and a few conventional apparatuses. First familiarize yourself with the simple recipes, which require the basic utensils, have fun with them, and enjoy them. When ready to venture to the more complex recipes, it is time to acquire the essential conventional apparatuses. You can purchase or order them in Sri Lankan grocery stores. *Idly* molds are more readily available in Indian grocery stores.

A range of saucepans (preferably nonstick)

Skillet

Deep saucepan for deep-frying

Slotted spoon

Sharp knife

Heat dissipater

A range of bowls

Ovenproof clay pot

Coconut scraper

Small wok with lid (to make hoppers)

Medium nonstick crepe pan

Steamer

Pestle and mortar or coffee grinder

Idly mold and a saucepan with lid (ensure the mold can be enclosed in the pan)

Pressure cooker

Stringhopper maker and 12 stringhopper *vatti* or molds

Conventional *pittu* apparatus

Kokis mold

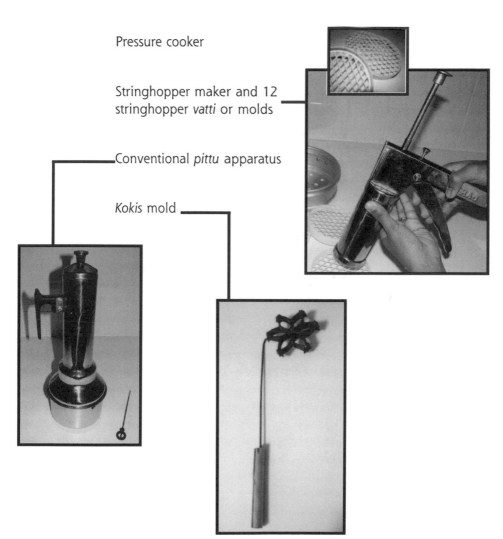

Measurements and Suggestions

For successful recipes, the following assumptions have been made with elements redefined. These clarifications and suggestions enable the recipes to be accurate and user-friendly.

1 cup liquid measure = 240ml
(water, milk, stock, etc.)

1 cup dry measure = 240ml
(Rice, flour, grated coconut, etc.)

1 tablespoon = 15ml
1 teaspoon = 5ml
$1/2$ teaspoon = 2ml

1 cup coconut milk
= 1 cup water + 4 to 5 teaspoons coconut milk powder
= 1 cup water + 4 to 5 tablespoons canned coconut milk

1 cup thick coconut milk
= 1 cup 2% milk + 4 to 5 teaspoons coconut milk powder
= 1 cup 2% milk + 4 tablespoons canned coconut milk

A small, moderately small, medium, and large saucepan would respectively correspond to an approximately 7, 9, 10, and 12-inch wide saucepan. The pan size influences the cooking times and required liquid measures of a recipe.

Sri Lankan foods are generally hot and spicy. Most recipes can be successfully toned down to a milder heat and made palatable to be enjoyed by all.

- Chili powder can be substituted with paprika powder, to achieve a hint of heat and classic hue.
- Other heat-inducing ingredients such as red chili flakes and curry powders can be reduced to $1/8$ of the original quantity.

- Green chilies and dry red chilies can be used whole (as the heat is not fully released until it's broken, or trace amounts can be used, or omit from the recipe.

When using an open flame as a heat source for cooking, it is best to use a heat dissipater to ensure even cooking. This also allows for more accurate cooking times. The use of a heat dissipater is highly recommended when making sweet-meats.

When describing a stock as mild, a less intense, lightly flavored clear broth is implied.

APPETIZERS

In Sri Lankan cuisine, appetizers are more commonly
referred to as short eats. A diverse array of mouthwatering savory treats
falls under this broad canopy. Short eats not only make great starters,
they are also popular served at teatime and make welcome snacks.

Chicken Patties

Makes 20

Enjoyed by children and adults alike, patties are an all-time favorite in Sri Lankan households.

In a moderately small nonstick saucepan combine the oil, onion, curry leaves, garlic, ginger, chili powder, curry powder, and turmeric powder. Fry on high heat for approximately 30 seconds and season with salt and pepper. Stir constantly to prevent burning.

Add the chicken, potato, and 1 tablespoon fennel leaves. Cook for another 40 to 50 seconds. Stir constantly and adjust salt. Add $3/4$ cup water, bring to a boil, cover and simmer on moderate heat for approximately 8 minutes. Adjust salt and stir occasionally.

Add the coconut milk and remaining fennel leaves. Cook uncovered on high heat for 4 to 6 minutes. Make sure the chicken is cooked through. If not add a little water and cook for another 1 to 2 minutes. When ready the mixture will come together. (Ideally the potato pieces should retain some of their shape.) Turn off heat, cover, and cool to room temperature.

In a medium bowl combine the flour, salt, and baking powder. Mix well to evenly distribute the ingredients. With the fingertips rub in the butter lightly and incorporate to form a flaky mixture. Season the water with lime. Make a well in the center of the flour and gradually add the water. Mix quickly and lightly to form the patty pastry. Avoid overworking the pastry. Cover and let rest for 5 to 10 minutes.

On a lightly floured flat surface roll out the pastry until quite thin and cut out approximately 4-inch rounds. Wet the edges of the rounds with water or egg white, place about 1 teaspoon of the filling in the center of each, fold over and press the edges together to seal. For a decorative touch, simply make indentations along the sealed edges by gently pressing the tines of a fork along it.

Heat the oil and fry the patties on moderately high heat until golden brown. Drain the excess oil on plenty of absorbent paper.

Variation

Fish makes a delicious alternative to chicken. This chicken filling can be successfully substituted by the fish filling described for Stuffed Fried Capsicums (page 37). When substituting, stir in 1 to 2 tablespoons of coconut milk to the cooked mixture and cook for another few seconds until absorbed by the mixture.

1 tablespoon vegetable oil
1 small onion, finely chopped
3 curry leaves
2 to 3 large cloves garlic, ground to a paste
1/2 to 1 teaspoon finely ground fresh ginger
1 1/2 teaspoons chili powder
1/4 to 1/2 teaspoon roasted Sinhala curry powder
Pinch to 1/8 teaspoon turmeric powder
Salt to taste
Freshly milled black pepper to taste
Meat of 3 chicken thighs, finely cubed
1 medium potato, peeled and finely cubed
2 tablespoons chopped fennel leaves
1/4 cup coconut milk
2 cups all-purpose flour
1 teaspoon salt
1/2 to 1 teaspoon baking powder
8 tablespoons cold butter, cut into small cubes
1/2 cup cold water
Fresh lime juice to taste
Oil for deep-frying

Savory Fish Cutlets

Always welcome, fish cutlets are delectable treats that are fantastic served as a finger-food and are equally special accompanying traditional Sri Lankan rice and curry meals. When these spicy cutlets take on the shape of large patties, they are best served with warm rustic bread, Dhal Curry (page 119), and Coconut Sambol (page 58).

Drain the liquid and remove any bones and impurities from the canned fish. With a fork or fingers, gently mash the fish. Sprinkle a pinch of salt over the cut green chilies. Heat the oil in a medium skillet. Add the onion, green chilies, turmeric powder, mustard seeds, and curry leaves. Fry for 40 to 50 seconds on high heat and stir continuously.

Add the garlic, fish, potatoes, pepper, and chili powder if using. Season with salt and, stirring frequently, fry for approximately 2 minutes. Mix in the lime juice and cook for a few more seconds. Adjust salt. When ready the mix will come together.

Once the mixture has cooled a little, using your hands form approximately 1 1/4-inch rounds (good when serving with rice or as a finger-food). If serving the cutlets with bread (as a dinner entrée), form the mixture into approximately 2 1/2-inch-round by 3/4-inch-high patties (makes 8 to 10).

To make the batter, in a small bowl combine the flour and 1 to 1 1/4 cups cold water. Mix well and season to taste with salt, pepper, and turmeric powder. Dip the fish rounds or patties in the batter, cover with bread crumbs, and deep-fry in batches until golden brown. Drain the excess oil on plenty of absorbent paper.

Tip
The cutlets can be made 2 to 3 days in advance, kept refrigerated (best uncovered), and deep-fried prior to serving.

1 (15-ounce) can jack mackerel
Salt to taste
4 medium green chilies, finely chopped
1 to 1 1/2 tablespoon vegetable oil
1 medium red onion, finely chopped
1/4 to 1/2 teaspoon turmeric powder
1/2 teaspoon mustard seeds
6 large curry leaves, finely sliced
1 large clove garlic, ground to a paste
2 large potatoes, boiled, peeled, and mashed
1 1/2 to 2 teaspoons freshly milled black pepper
1/2 to 1 teaspoon chili powder or Jaffna curry powder (optional)
Fresh lime juice to taste
1 cup all-purpose flour
1 1/2 to 2 cups coarse bread crumbs
Oil for deep-frying

Stuffed Fried Capsicums

Makes 8 to 10

The simple fish filling makes an ideal partner to the capsicum, while the contrasting yet complementary texture and flavors of the crispy cover and succulent filling completes this recipe.

When choosing the capsicums for presentation it is nice to pick ones with stems attached. Place the whole capsicums in a medium saucepan, cover with water, and season with a little salt. Bring to a boil, cook for 1½ to 2 minutes, and turn off heat. Cover and leave for a few minutes. Once cooled to room temperature cut each capsicum lengthwise on one side and carefully scoop out and discard the seeds and white lining.

Drain the fish and remove the skin and bones. Break the fish into small pieces. Heat the oil in a medium saucepan and fry the onion, green chili, and curry leaves for approximately 20 seconds. Stir frequently to prevent burning.

Add the fish, turmeric powder, chili powder, and garlic if using. Season with salt and pepper and cook on moderate heat for 1 to 2 minutes. Stir constantly. Add the potato and, gently mashing the ingredients with the spoon, cook for another 1 to 2 minutes. Adjust salt and pepper. When ready the mixture will come together. Turn off heat and stir in the lime juice. Let cool to room temperature.

Fill the capsicums with the fish mixture. In a medium bowl (oval-shaped dish is best) combine the flour and water. Mix well and season with salt, pepper, and turmeric powder. Carefully dip the capsicums one at a time in the batter (ensure that they are entirely covered in batter) and cover with bread crumbs. Pat the bread crumbs on well.

8 to 10 medium capsicums
Salt to taste
½ (15-ounce) can jack mackerel
1 tablespoon vegetable oil
1 small onion, finely chopped
1 to 2 medium green chilies, finely chopped
3 curry leaves, sliced
Pinch to ⅛ teaspoon turmeric powder
½ to ¾ teaspoon chili powder
1 to 2 large cloves garlic, ground to a paste (optional)
Plenty of freshly milled black pepper
1 medium potato, boiled, peeled, and mashed
Fresh lime juice to taste
1 cup all-purpose flour
1 to 1¼ cups cold water
1½ to 2 cups coarse bread crumbs
Oil for deep-frying

Heat the oil and fry the capsicums in batches until golden brown. Drain the excess oil on plenty of absorbent paper. Best served warm. Also good served with rice and curry.

Ulunthu Vadai

Makes 10

Also known as *Masala Vadai*, these are urad dhal-based doughnut-shaped savories traditionally of Indian origin.

Soak the urad dhal in water for 4 hours. Drain and grind to a smooth puree. Transfer to a medium bowl.

Add the fennel seeds, curry leaves, onion, and green chilies. Mix well to evenly distribute the ingredients. Prior to frying, season well with salt. (The unseasoned mixture can be stored in an airtight container in the refrigerator for 2 to 3 days.)

Heat the oil in a wide-mouthed frying pan. Have at hand a bowl of cold water and a hand towel. Wet both palms and fingers with water, take approximately a 2-tablespoon portion of the mixture, and on the palm form into a doughnut shape. Promptly and carefully transfer into the oil. Repeat with the remaining mixture.

1 cup split urad dhal
1/4 teaspoon fennel seeds
8 curry leaves, finely
  chopped
3/4 to 1 medium onion, finely
  chopped
4 medium green chilies,
  finely chopped
Salt to taste
Oil for deep-frying

Cook the *vadai* in batches on moderate heat, until cooked through and golden brown. Turn the *vadai* over during cooking. (Immediately reduce heat if the oil is too hot and the vadai burns on impact.) Drain the excess oil on plenty of absorbent paper. Let rest for 5 to 10 minutes and serve while still warm.

Ulunthu Vadai is served with green chili and coriander chutney, Coconut Sambol (page 58), or Mint Sambol (page 59).

Tip
A cheat method to forming the "doughnut" holes until the traditional method is mastered is to transfer the rounded portions into the hot oil and immediately and carefully pierce through the centers with a wooden spoon.

Thatta Vadai

Makes 20 to 24

Surprisingly simple to prepare, these flat crisps are a perfect blend of urad dhal, fennel, curry leaves, and chili. *Thatta Vadai* is a unique Tamil recipe that makes an addictive snack.

Soak the urad dhal in water for 1½ hours. Drain and transfer to a medium bowl.

Stir in the fennel seeds, curry leaves, flour, and chili powder. Mix thoroughly to evenly distribute the ingredients. Prior to frying season well with salt.

Heat the oil. Divide the mixture into portions and form into balls. Have at hand a bowl of cold water and a hand towel. Wet the palm and fingers, place a ball on the palm, and flatten into very thin (1 layer of the dhal) rounds. Briskly and carefully transfer into the oil and fry until golden brown and crispy.

Drain the excess oil on plenty of absorbent paper. Let cool to room temperature before serving. *Thatta Vadai* will keep for over a week stored in an airtight container at room temperature.

1 cup split urad dhal
3 teaspoons fennel seeds
15 to 20 curry leaves, chopped
½ to ⅔ cup all-purpose flour
½ to ⅔ teaspoon chili powder
Salt to taste
Oil for deep-frying

Meat-Filled Capsicums

The capsicum halves are filled with a delicately spiced meat and potato filling and encased in a delicious egg batter that is fried to golden perfection.

When choosing the capsicums for presentation it is nice to pick ones with stems attached. Place the whole capsicums in a medium saucepan, cover with water, and season with a little salt. Bring to a boil, cook for 1½ to 2 minutes, and turn off heat. Cover and leave for a few minutes. Once cooled to room temperature cut each capsicum lengthwise into halves (also along the stem) and carefully scoop out and discard the seeds and white lining.

In a moderately small nonstick saucepan, combine the meat, oil, onion, tomato, and vinegar. Season with salt, pepper, turmeric powder, and chili powder if using and cook on moderately high heat for approximately 3 minutes. Mix in the potato and adjust salt and pepper. Cook for another few seconds and stir constantly until the mixture comes together and maintains a moist consistency. Cool the mixture to room temperature.

Fill the capsicum halves with the mixture. Form and shape the mixture to mimic the capsicum other half (the final shape should be of a whole capsicum). Make the batter in a medium oval-shaped dish by combing the flour, egg, and water. Mix well to form a smooth thick batter and season with salt, pepper, and turmeric powder. If the batter is too thick, add 1 to 3 teaspoons water.

3 to 4 medium capsicums
8 ounces ground beef
1 to 2 teaspoons vegetable oil
1 small onion, finely chopped
½ to 1 small tomato, finely chopped
½ teaspoon vinegar
Salt to taste
Plenty of freshly milled black pepper to taste
Pinch to ⅛ teaspoon turmeric powder
Chili powder to taste (optional)
1 medium potato, boiled, peeled, and mashed
½ cup all-purpose flour
1 extra large egg, beaten
¼ cup water
Oil for deep-frying

Heat the oil. Carefully coat the capsicums with batter and fry until golden brown. Drain the excess oil on plenty of absorbent paper. Let rest for a few minutes before serving.

Potato Balls

Ala Bola   *Makes 10*

Ala bola is in essence a beautifully spiced potato and cashew filling coated in a thick flour batter that is fried to a crispy golden brown.

Peel and roughly mash the potatoes into a chunky consistency. If using cashews pre-soak in water for 24 hours (change the water 3 times during this period). Heat the oil in a medium pan. Add the onion and curry leaves and cook on moderately high heat for 30 to 40 seconds. Stir in the cashews if using, turmeric powder, mustard seeds, green chili, and maldive fish if using. Cook for approximately 20 seconds. Stir frequently to prevent burning.

Add the potato and chili powder and season with salt. Stirring constantly, cook on moderately low heat for 1 to 2 minutes until the mixture comes together. Adjust salt and turmeric powder. Take off the heat and while still warm divide the mixture into 10. Form the portions into balls.

Make the thick batter by combining the flour and baking powder in a medium bowl. Add the water, mix well, and season with salt and a pinch of turmeric powder.

Heat the oil. Cover the potato balls in batter and fry on moderately high heat until golden brown. Drain the excess oil on plenty of absorbent paper. Best served immediately while warm and crispy.

Variation

For a difference make the batter substituting besan flour (gram flour) for the chana flour. Once fried this will result in a softer slightly spongy textured cover.

2 medium potatoes, boiled
1/4 cup cashew nut pieces
   (optional)
1 to 1 1/2 tablespoons
   vegetable oil
1 small onion, finely
   chopped
6 to 8 curry leaves, chopped
1/8 teaspoon turmeric powder
1 teaspoon mustard seeds
4 medium green chilies,
   finely chopped
1/2 to 1 teaspoon maldive
   fish flakes (optional)
1/2 teaspoon chili powder
Salt to taste
1 1/3 cup chana flour (*ata*
   flour)
1/4 teaspoon baking powder
2/3 cup iced or cold water
Oil for deep-frying

Mutton Rolls

Makes 16 to 18

A beautiful spiced mutton and potato dry curry is rolled in a delicate crepe, dipped in batter, breaded and fried to golden perfection. These rolls also make a welcome dinner entrée.

In a moderately small nonstick saucepan combine the oil, meat, potato, onion, green chilies, garlic, ginger, curry leaves, turmeric powder, chili powder, Jaffna curry powder, Sinhala curry powder if using, vinegar if using, and approximately 1 cup water. Bring to a boil and season with salt and pepper. Cover and simmer on moderate heat for 10 to 12 minutes. Cook uncovered for another few minutes until the mixture comes together. Adjust salt, pepper, and chili powder and stir constantly. Make sure the meat is cooked. (If not done add a little water and cook for a few minutes.) Let the mixture cool a little.

In a medium bowl combine $1\frac{1}{4}$ cups flour, the egg, butter if using, and approximately $2\frac{1}{4}$ cups water. Mix well to make a smooth batter and season with salt. Heat a small nonstick pan, lightly grease it, and pour a small portion of the batter to make an approximately 7-inch very thin crepe. Cook on moderate heat for 25 to 30 seconds (until the edges begin to slightly lift off the pan) and adjust heat to prevent overcooking and over-coloring.

Transfer to a plate and while still warm place about 2 teaspoons of the filling in a line approximately $\frac{1}{3}$ inch from the edge. Fold the two ends perpendicular to the filling in and roll tight beginning with the end closest to the filling. It is imperative that this be done quickly, while the crepe is still warm. (If the seam does not stick because the crepe has been overcooked, use egg white as glue.) Set aside seam side down until all the crepes are made and stuffed.

Make the batter for frying in a medium bowl by combining the remaining flour with approximately $1^3/_4$ to 2 cups cold water. Mix well and season with salt, pepper, and turmeric powder. Dip the rolls (one at a time) in the batter and cover with bread crumbs. Heat the oil and deep-fry until golden brown. Drain the excess oil on plenty of absorbent paper.

Variation
The fish filling used for Stuffed Fried Capsicums (page 37) makes a successful substitution to the meat filling in this recipe.

Tip
The batter for frying can be effectively substituted with a few beaten eggs simply brushed over the rolls.

1 to 3 teaspoons vegetable oil
8 ounces ground mutton or lamb
1 medium potato, peeled and finely cubed
1 small onion, finely chopped
2 medium green chilies, finely chopped
2 to 3 large cloves garlic, ground to a paste
1 to 2 teaspoons finely ground fresh ginger
6 curry leaves
Pinch to $^1/_8$ teaspoon turmeric powder
1 teaspoon chili powder
$1^1/_2$ to 2 teaspoons Jaffna curry powder
$^1/_4$ teaspoon roasted Sinhala curry powder (optional)
$^1/_2$ teaspoon vinegar (optional)
Salt to taste
Plenty of freshly milled black pepper to taste
$2^1/_4$ cups all-purpose flour
1 extra large egg, beaten
1 to 2 tablespoons butter, melted (optional)
1 to 2 cups coarse bread crumbs
Oil for deep-frying

Fish Buns

For many generations *Maalu Paan* has been equally popular both as a teatime snack and a quick lunch.

Remove the skin and bones and crush the fish into a fairly smooth consistency. Heat the oil in a medium pan. Add the leeks, curry leaves, mustard seeds, green chilies, turmeric powder, and carrot if using. Fry for approximately 30 seconds on high heat and stir frequently to prevent burning.

Add the fish and potato. Season with chili powder, salt and pepper. Cook on moderate heat for 2 to 3 minutes and stir frequently. Add the coconut milk, adjust salt and pepper, and cook for another few seconds until the mixture comes together. (As well as adding flavor, the milk moistens the mixture.) Season with lime juice. Cover and cool to room temperature.

In a medium bowl combine the yeast and sugar. Mix well and stir in the warm milk. It is imperative that the milk is not hot but warm, as it will otherwise kill and render the yeast inactive. Ensure that the yeast and sugar are well mixed with the milk. Set aside.

In a large bowl combine the flour and salt. Mix well to evenly distribute the salt. Add the yeast mixture into the center of the flour and mix lightly. Gradually add the water, forming a soft dough, and mix in the butter. Form into a ball. Place the dough in a greased (2 to 3 teaspoons oil) medium bowl, loosely cover with plastic wrap, and let stand in a warm place for 15 minutes.

Turn the dough onto a floured surface and knead (pushing and pulling and adding a little flour if necessary) well for about 6 minutes. Grease a medium bowl well, using 1 to 1½ tablespoons oil, and place the dough in it. Turn the dough over once to coat with oil, loosely cover with plastic wrap, and leave in a warm place for 20 minutes.

Preheat the oven to 400°F. Take portions of the risen dough, stretch and fill with the fish mixture, and close to envelope the filling. Press well and form into rounds or the traditional triangular shapes. (There will be a little mixture left over.) Place seam side down on a baking tray (preferably lined with parchment paper), position on the center rack, and bake for 15 to 20 minutes. When ready the buns will have lightly colored tops and emit a slightly hollow sound when tapped. Set aside and let cool a bit before serving. They are good served at room temperature too.

Variation

For a vegetarian alternative, fill portions of dough prepared as described above with *Seeni Sambol* (page 69). Ensure the buns are well sealed as the *Seeni Sambol* is slightly oily and tends to seep out during baking.

1 (15-ounce) can jack mackerel (can use canned tuna, cooked fish)
1 tablespoon vegetable oil
1 tightly packed cup finely sliced leeks
10 small to medium curry leaves
⅛ teaspoon mustard seeds
5 medium green chilies, finely chopped
Pinch to ⅛ teaspoon turmeric powder
1 tablespoon grated carrot (optional)
1 medium potato, boiled, peeled, and mashed
½ to 1 teaspoon chili powder
Salt to taste
Plenty of freshly milled black pepper to taste
1 to 2 tablespoons coconut milk or 2% milk
Fresh lime juice to taste
¾ teaspoon active dry yeast
½ teaspoon sugar
¾ cup warm 2% milk
4 cups all-purpose flour
1 to 1½ teaspoons salt
1 cup warm water
1 to 1¼ tablespoons butter or margarine, at room temperature

Stuffed Godamba Roti

These highly presentable delicious parcels of spiced fish and potato are a welcome treat to the taste buds. Stuffed *Godamba Roti* make excellent appetizers and teatime snacks.

Drain and save the fish liquid. Remove the skin and bones of the fish and separate the fish into slightly chunky flakes. (Traditionally this recipe calls for boiled fresh kingfish.)

Heat the oil in a medium nonstick saucepan. Add the onion, green chilies, curry leaves, turmeric powder, and mustard seeds. Season with salt and cook on moderate heat until the onions have sweated. Stir occasionally to prevent burning.

Add the fish, pepper, chili powder, and potato. Adjust salt, add 1 to 2 teaspoons of the fish liquid as necessary, and cook on moderate heat for another 2 to 3 minutes. Stir frequently. Season with lime juice if using. Cover and let cool to room temperature.

Place a portion of dough on a flat surface (a plate would suffice) and with the fingers push and stretch to form a paper-thin square. Place a portion of the filling (in a square shape) in the center. Fold the dough to envelopes the filling and form a tight, square parcel. Do the same with the remaining dough and filling.

Heat a medium or large preferably nonstick pan. Cook the parcels (on all sides beginning with the seam side down) on moderately low heat until golden brown. Make sure the dough is cooked through. Best served warm.

1 (15-ounce) can jack mackerel
1 tablespoons vegetable oil
1 medium onion, finely chopped
4 to 5 medium green chilies, finely chopped
8 curry leaves
Pinch to 1/8 teaspoon turmeric powder
1/4 teaspoon mustard seeds
Salt to taste
1/2 to 3/4 teaspoon freshly milled black pepper
1/4 to 1/2 teaspoon chili powder
1 medium potato, boiled, peeled, and roughly chopped
Fresh lime juice to taste (optional)
Godamba Roti dough, divided in 8 (page 93)

Minced Beef Pastries

These sumptuous puff pastry-encased delicately spiced meat pastries are tremendous when accompanied with a hot cup of freshly brewed tea.

Thaw the pastry. It takes approximately 30 minutes at room temperature.

Heat the oil in a medium nonstick saucepan. Add the onion, potato, curry leaves, turmeric powder, green chilies, garlic, and ginger. Fry on moderately high heat for approximately 3 minutes and stir constantly.

Add the beef, curry powder, and chili powder if using. Season with salt and pepper and cook for another minute. Stir frequently. Add about 1 1/4 cups water, cover, and cook on moderately high heat for approximately 12 minutes, until the water is absorbed and the potato and meat are cooked.

Stir in the coconut milk, adjust salt, and cook on high for 15 to 20 seconds. Stir constantly. Turn off heat and let the mixture cool to room temperature. If the pastry is filled while the mixture is hot or too warm it will melt and lose its integrity. Preheat the oven to 400°F (or if otherwise stated in package instructions, to that temperature).

Cut the pastry into approximately 3 1/2-inch squares and place a portion of the filling in the center. Fold over to form either triangles or rectangle (it is nice to differentiate when two types of fillings are used) and seal the edges by pressing firmly or use an egg wash as glue. Place on a baking sheet (preferably lined with parchment paper) and brush the pastry tops with the egg. Bake until golden brown (approximately 20 minutes) and the pastry is nice and puffed.

1 (1.1-pound) package frozen puff pastry (two 10 1/2 by 10 1/2-inch sheets)
2 tablespoons vegetable oil
1 small onion, finely chopped
1 medium potato, peeled and finely cubed
3 curry leaves, sliced
Pinch to 1/8 teaspoon turmeric powder
1 to 2 medium green chilies, finely chopped
1 to 2 large cloves garlic, ground to a paste
1/2 teaspoon finely ground or grated ginger
3/4 pound ground beef
3/4 to 1 tablespoon Jaffna curry powder
1/2 to 1 teaspoon chili powder (optional)
Salt to taste
Freshly milled black pepper to taste
1 tablespoon thick coconut milk (see page 31)
1 large egg, beaten

Stir-fried Chickpeas with Coconut

Serves 4 to 6

This mouthwatering preparation is highly flavorful and extremely simple to concoct. The flavor and texture of the brown chickpeas are perfectly complemented by that of the coconut, dry red chili, and mustard seeds.

Soak the chickpeas overnight (8 to 10 hours) in water. (This considerably reduces cooking time.) Boil the chickpeas in plenty of well-salted water until cooked and tender. For 10 hours of soaking the boiling time is approximately 30 minutes. Drain well.

Heat the oil in a medium saucepan. Add the onion if using and fry until golden. Add the chilies, curry leaves, mustard seeds, turmeric powder if using, and coconut. Season with salt and fry on moderately high heat until the chilies are browned and the coconut colored. Stir constantly.

Add the chickpeas and cook on high heat for approximately 1 minute. Stir constantly and adjust salt. This quick and delicious recipe also makes a great breakfast.

2 cups dry brown chickpeas (*konda kadala*)
1 tablespoon vegetable oil
1 small red onion, finely sliced (optional)
10 to 12 whole dry red chilies, broken into $1/2$ to $3/4$-inch pieces
10 small curry leaves
1 to $1 1/8$ teaspoon mustard seeds
Pinch to $1/8$ teaspoon turmeric powder (optional)
$1/4$ to $1/3$ cup tooth-size pieces fresh coconut
Salt to taste
Freshly milled black pepper to taste (optional)

Tips

We typically use the brown chickpeas in this recipe but the yellow variety could be used successful. For a quicker result (as no soaking and boiling of the chickpeas is required) canned chickpeas can be used.

Rehydrated desiccated coconut can be substituted for the fresh coconut pieces in this recipe.

Vegetable Sandwiches

Makes 20 to 24

An absolute favorite of mine, these unique colorful layered sandwiches combine beetroot with carrot. The inherent goodness of the vegetables is accentuated by a medley of creative ingredients.

In a small bowl, mix the pureed carrots and 1/4 cup cream cheese. Season the pureed beetroots with salt, and place in the center of a piece of muslin or other porous cloth. With the hand, gather the ends of the cloth and tighten to squeeze out excess water (that would make the sandwiches soggy) from the beetroots. Transfer the beetroots to a small bowl and stir in the remaining 1/4 cup cream cheese.

Sprinkle a pinch of salt over the green chilies and add them to the beetroot mixture. Mix well and season with salt, pepper, and sugar if using.

Combine the cumin, coriander, and mustard seeds in a mortar, grind finely, and add to the carrot mixture. Mix well and season with salt, pepper and sugar if using. Mix in the parsley. Refrigerate both the carrot and the beetroot spreads for about 30 minutes before assembling the sandwiches. This allows the flavors to unify and the mixtures to slightly solidify and become less runny.

Arrange the bread in three-slice stacks. (A day or so old bread makes it easier to cut the sandwiches.) Generously butter the top of the bottom slice, top and bottom of the middle slice, and bottom of the top slice of each stack. Spread the beetroot mixture on the bottom slice and place the middle slice over it. Spread the carrot mixture over that and cover with the top slice, with the buttered side facing down.

1 cup coarsely pureed boiled carrots (about 8 ounces)
1/2 cup cream cheese
1 cup coarsely pureed boiled beetroots (about 8 ounces)
Salt to taste
3 medium green chilies, finely chopped
Freshly milled black pepper to taste
Pinch of sugar (optional)
1/4 teaspoon cumin seeds, lightly pan-roasted
1/4 teaspoon coriander seeds, pan-roasted
1 1/3 teaspoons mustard seeds
1 to 2 tablespoons finely chopped fresh parsley
15 to 18 slices white sandwich bread
Butter spread

Place on a cutting board and carefully trim (with a sharp knife) the four edges. Have a damp cloth or paper towel handy to wipe off, in between cuts, any colored mixture that might be on the knife. Carefully cut into 4 squares. Fill and cut the remaining stacks of bread. Cover with a damp, clean cloth or paper towel (it helps prevent the bread from drying out) and refrigerate. Best served slightly cool.

Batter-Fried Anchovies

Anchovies probably never tasted better than prepared according to this uncomplicated recipe. Red chili and black pepper add a zing to this preparation that is laced with a perfect hint of zesty lime.

Cut the fish heads off, gut, wash and clean well. Place the fish in a medium bowl. Add the lime rind, chili powder, and pepper. Season with salt and mix well.

Make the batter in a separate medium bowl by combining the flour, milk, egg, and turmeric powder. Mix well to achieve a smooth consistency and season with salt and plenty of pepper. Pour the batter ($^1/_3$ to $^1/_2$ quantity should suffice) into the bowl with the seasoned fish and mix well. Adjust salt, pepper, chili powder, and lime.

Heat the oil. Deep-fry in batches, on moderately high heat until golden brown. Turn the fish over during cooking. Drain the excess oil on plenty of absorbent paper. Adjust salt and chili (sprinkle if more is needed) and drizzle a good squeeze of lime while hot. Best served immediately. This recipe also works well with other small fish like small sardines and smelt, as well as with prawns.

25 to 30 large fresh anchovies
$^1/_4$ to $^1/_2$ teaspoon finely grated lime zest or fresh lime juice to taste
$^1/_2$ teaspoon chili powder
$^1/_2$ to 1 teaspoon freshly milled black pepper
Salt to taste
1 cup all-purpose flour
1 cup cold 2% milk
1 large egg
$^1/_4$ to $^1/_3$ teaspoon turmeric powder
Oil for deep-frying

Prawns Wrapped in Spicy Pastry

Makes 20

A wonderfully warm and rich spiced pastry transforms the delicate flavors of the sea by introducing a dimension of crispy texture and subtle heat.

In a medium bowl combine the flour, salt, 1 teaspoon chili powder, pinch of turmeric powder, and cumin. Mix well to evenly distribute the ingredients. Using your fingers, lightly rub in the butter to form a crumbly texture.

1 cup all-purpose flour
$1/2$ teaspoon salt
$1/4$ teaspoon baking powder
$2^1/2$ to $2^3/4$ teaspoons chili powder
Pinch to $1/8$ teaspoon turmeric powder
$1/4$ teaspoon ground cumin
4 tablespoons cold butter, cut into small pieces
Fresh lime juice to taste
$1/4$ cup cold water
20 medium tiger prawns
1 to $1^1/2$ teaspoons vinegar
Freshly milled black pepper to taste
Oil for deep-frying

Mix the lime juice with the water and gradually add the water to the flour. Mix to form the pastry. The pastry should not have any cracks. Avoid overworking the pastry. Cover and let rest for 5 to 10 minutes.

Remove the prawn heads and shells, with the exception of the tail shells, and de-vein the prawns. Place in a small bowl and season with salt, lime juice, vinegar, $1^1/2$ to $1^3/4$ teaspoons chili powder, turmeric powder, and pepper. Mix well and set aside.

On a lightly floured surface roll the pastry out into a very thin sheet. With a sharp knife cut into approximately $1/2$ by 12-inch strips. Lightly brush the surface of a strip with water. Starting with the tail end (with about $2/3$ of the tail shell showing) tightly wrap the pastry strip along the length of the prawn. With each round, overlap about half of the previous round and press firmly to secure. Seal the pastry at the head-end by pressing firmly to form a stump. Gently rub the marinade over the wrapped pastry.

Heat the oil and deep-fry the prawns on moderately high heat until golden brown. Ensure the prawns are cooked through. Drain the excess oil on plenty of absorbent paper. Let rest a few minutes before serving. Can be served warm or at room temperature.

Pineapple-Cheese-Liver-Onion Sticks

Makes 40

This recipe calls for a combination of flavors and textures to create the perfect bite. It is extremely simple to prepare.

In a small saucepan combine the onions and 1 1/2 cups vinegar. Season with salt and parboil the onions. Drain and let cool.

Boil the liver in water seasoned with salt, pepper, turmeric powder, and 1 tablespoon vinegar. Let cool and cut into approximately 1/2-inch cubes (need 40 pieces). Combine the liver pieces and margarine in a medium nonstick pan and cook on moderately high heat to slightly color the pieces. Stir frequently to prevent burning and adjust salt and pepper.

Ensure the pineapple chunks are approximately 1/2-inch cubes. Cut the cheese into approximately 1/2-inch cubes.

Leaving the head on, cut a slice off the stem end to form a base and peel the pineapple. Stand the pineapple on a plate. Assemble a piece each of the pineapple, cheese, liver, and onion on a toothpick and stick the units on the pineapple body (for presentation).

40 red pearl onions
1 1/2 cups plus 1 tablespoon
   vinegar
Salt to taste
1/3 pound beef liver
Freshly milled black pepper
   to taste
Pinch to 1/8 teaspoon
   turmeric powder
2 tablespoons margarine
1 (20-ounce) can
   pineapple chunks, drained
5 ounces cheddar cheese
1 small pineapple
Toothpicks (need
   approximately 4-inch
   skewers)

SALADS

The Sri Lankan interpretation and role of a salad are delightfully diverse from that of the western world. A "salad" is a delicious blend of flavors that tie the elements of a meal together and is an essential component of the Sri Lankan menu. It is rarely a meal in itself and is often considered a side dish. Salads are presented with many faces, be it in the form of a unique *sambol*, cooked *mallum* or raw *saladé*. These traditional and popular recipes are made from a variety of ingredients ranging from the most humble to the more exotic and served both warm and cold.

Traditional Eggplant Salad

Serves 4

This unique Sri Lankan salad is a welcome addition to any meal. In this recipe, the tangy flavor of lemon and the heat of the green chilies delightfully complement the earthy goodness of the eggplant. well. When using the non-Asian variety of eggplant, it is advisable to cut out and discard some of the spongy core, as it tends to absorb a lot of oil during frying. Let the eggplant pieces marinate for approximately 5 minutes.

Heat the oil in a medium saucepan. Deep-fry the eggplant in batches, being careful to avoid overcrowding the pan. When ready, the eggplant should be a beautiful golden brown hue. Drain the excess oil on plenty of absorbent paper.

Place the chopped green chilies in a small bowl and sprinkle a pinch of salt over them. Let the salted chilies rest until the eggplant is cooked.

Cut the eggplant into approximately $2\frac{1}{2}$ by $\frac{1}{2}$-inch pieces, sprinkle on the turmeric powder, and mix

1 to 2 medium green chilies, chopped
Salt to taste
2 medium Asian eggplants or 1 medium eggplant ($\frac{3}{4}$ to 1 pound)
$\frac{1}{8}$ teaspoon turmeric powder
Oil for deep-frying
1 medium red onion, finely sliced
$\frac{1}{2}$ to 1 teaspoon maldive fish flakes (optional)
Fresh lime juice to taste
Freshly milled black pepper to taste

In a separate bowl combine the fried eggplant, onion, maldive fish flakes if using, lime juice, and green chilies. Mix well to evenly distribute and incorporate all flavors. Season to taste with salt and black pepper. Best served with steamed white rice.

Vegetable Rainbow Salad

This simple yet elegant and wonderfully harmonious recipe spans the colors of the rainbow. This attractive salad is possibly the sole exception to the "Sri Lankan salad rule," for it truly could be a meal in itself.

Slice the beetroots and tomatoes into approximately ½-inch-thick rounds and cut the carrots into approximately ½-inch cubes.

Peel the cucumber and run the tines of a fork down the length of it. These striated markings will leave a decorative edge when the cucumber is sliced. Slice the cucumber into approximately ⅓-inch-thick rounds.

Slice the onions into fairly thick rounds. Separate the onion rounds into rings (optional) and the lettuce into individual leafs. Arrange the salad leaves to decoratively cover the base of a serving platter. Season with salt and pepper.

Form little bundles by stacking a slice each of beetroot, tomato, cucumber, and onion. Place the vegetable bundles on the salad leaves and sprinkle on the carrots. Season with salt and pepper.

2 medium beetroots, boiled
2 medium firm tomatoes
2 medium carrots, boiled
1 large cucumber
2 medium red onions
1 small head lettuce
   (preferably green-leaf
   lettuce)
Salt to taste
Freshly milled black pepper
   to taste

Variation
The addition of 4 eggs, hard-boiled and cut lengthwise into quarters, will introduce an interesting element of flavor and texture to this colorful recipe.

Breadfruit Mallum

Serves 6

The beauty of this exquisite dish is in the simplicity of its preparation and the seductive charm of its key ingredient. This exotic warm salad that befits kings is guaranteed to whet the appetite.

Peel the thick green skin of the breadfruit. Cut the breadfruit into wedges and cut and discard the inedible core. Boil in salted water until a fork can be inserted effortlessly. Add a pinch of turmeric powder to the boiling water, as breadfruit has a tendency to discolor. Drain the water and cut the breadfruit into small pieces.

In a medium saucepan combine the coconut, green chilies, black pepper, $1/2$ teaspoon mustard seeds, and ground mustard if using. Pan-roast on high heat for approximately 40 seconds and stir constantly to prevent burning. Stir in the breadfruit and cook for another minute.

Heat the oil in a small pan. Add the onions and fry until golden. Add the curry leaves, the remaining mustard seeds, $1/8$ teaspoon turmeric powder, garlic, ginger, chili powder if using, black peppercorns, and dry chili pieces. Season with salt and fry for approximately 20 seconds. Stir in this mixture into the breadfruit. Cook for another 1 to 2 minutes on moderate heat. Adjust seasoning by adding salt if necessary.

1 young breadfruit ($1^1/2$ to 2 pounds)
Salt to taste
$1/8$ teaspoon plus a pinch turmeric powder
2 to 3 tablespoons grated coconut
2 medium green chilies, chopped
Black pepper to taste
$1^1/2$ teaspoons mustard seeds
$1/2$ to 1 teaspoon ground mustard (optional)
2 tablespoons vegetable oil
1 small red onion, finely sliced
6 to 8 curry leaves
1 to 2 cloves garlic, finely sliced
1 teaspoon finely chopped fresh ginger
$1/2$ teaspoon chili powder (optional)
6 black peppercorns
3 whole dry red chilies, broken into approximately $3/4$-inch pieces

Crispy Bitter Gourd Salad

Karavila Salad *Serves 4*

A touch of bitterness with a trace of sourness and a dash of spiciness make this bitter gourd salad especially intriguing. It is best served over steamed white rice and, as a native Sri Lankan would say, "it is a definite rice pusher."

Sprinkle a pinch of salt on the chopped green chilies and let stand for 2 to 3 minutes. Salting helps balance and round off the inherent heat of the chilies.

Cut the *karavila* into very thin slices (should yield approximately 2 tightly packed cups) and transfer to a medium bowl (make sure to include seeds that might fall off when the *karavila* is cut). For a crispier result, sprinkle 1 teaspoon salt and let stand for approximately 1 hour. Prior to frying, squeeze the *karavila* to extract the water and pat dry with a paper towel.

Salt to taste
1 to 2 medium green chilies, finely chopped
2 medium or 1 large Asian *karavila* (bitter gourds)
Oil for deep-frying
1 to 2 small red onions, finely chopped
1/2 teaspoon maldive fish flakes (optional)
Fresh lime juice to taste
Freshly milled black pepper to taste

Heat the oil in a medium saucepan and deep-fry in batches. When ready, the bitter gourd will be golden brown in color with a crispy texture. Drain the excess oil on absorbent paper.

In a medium bowl combine the red onion, green chilies, maldive fish if using, and lime. Add the fried *karavila*, mix well, and season with salt and black pepper. In order to preserve the crispy texture of the *karavila*, it is best to assemble this salad immediately prior to serving.

Variation
For a delightful difference in flavor, introduce a medium finely chopped tomato to the above recipe.

Coconut Sambol

Serves 4 to 6

The delicate taste of coconut and the fiery hotness of chili combine to make this unique *sambol*. This all-time Sri Lankan favorite is commonly referred to as *Pol Sambol* and is especially delicious served with steamed rice, Stringhoppers (page 89), or warm yeast bread. and blend all the ingredients thoroughly. Alternatively, place all the ingredients in a blender and pulse for a few seconds. The desired color for this *sambol* is a lovely red-orange. If using a lesser amount of chili, paprika powder could be added to aid in achieving the desired hue without compromising flavor.

Variation
Prepare the above *sambol*. Place it in a flat skillet and pan-roast on moderately high heat for 2 to 3 minutes. Stir constantly to prevent burning. For a further dimension of flavor add 1 to 2 fresh mint leaves.

Sprinkle a pinch of salt on the chopped green chilies and let the chilies rest for 2 to 3 minutes.

In a large mortar, combine the coconut, onion, chili powder, chili flakes, maldive fish if using, black pepper, garlic, ginger, curry leaves if using, lime juice, and green chilies. Mix thoroughly to incorporate all flavors and season with salt. With the pestle, pound to mix

Salt to taste
3 medium green chilies, finely chopped
2 cups grated coconut
1 medium red onion, finely chopped
2 teaspoons red chili powder
2 teaspoons red chili flakes
1/2 to 1 teaspoon maldive fish flakes (optional)
1/2 teaspoon freshly milled black pepper
3 cloves garlic, chopped
1 to 2 teaspoons finely chopped fresh ginger
5 curry leaves (optional)
Plenty of fresh lime juice to taste

Mint Sambol

Minchi Sambol

While the essence of this dish is the refreshing taste and aroma of fresh mint, the beautiful flavor and texture of the coconut is truly complementary and vital to its success. *Minchi Sambol* is best served with *Buriyani* (page 80).

Place in a mortar the *minchi*, onion, coconut, green chilies, lime juice, turmeric powder if using, garlic, and ginger. Season to taste with salt and pepper. Pound and grind with the pestle to thoroughly blend the ingredients. Alternatively, place the above ingredients in an electric blender and pulse for a few seconds.

Transfer the mint mixture to a medium skillet and pan-roast for 2 to 3 minutes on moderate heat. Stir constantly to prevent burning.

1 to 1½ cups tightly packed fresh *minchi* (mint) leaves and tender stalks

½ medium red onion, finely chopped

3 to 4 tablespoons grated coconut

5 medium green chilies, finely chopped

Juice of ½ to 1 lime

Pinch of turmeric powder (optional)

3 cloves garlic, ground

1 teaspoon finely chopped fresh ginger

Salt to taste

Freshly milled black pepper to taste

Coconut Mallum

Serves 2 to 3

This unique warm salad, commonly referred to as Stringhopper Sambol and *Pol Mallum*, is typically served with Stringhoppers (page 89).

In a small saucepan combine the onion, green chili, curry leaves, turmeric powder, mustard seeds, lime juice, ginger, garlic, cinnamon, peppercorns, maldive fish, and 1 cup water. Bring to a boil, season with salt and pepper, and boil for 2 to 3 minutes.

Add the coconut, adjust salt, and cook on high heat for 6 to 8 minutes. Stir occasionally. The final consistency of this preparation should be moist.

1 small red onion, finely chopped
1 small green chili, cut in half
3 curry leaves
$1/8$ teaspoon turmeric powder
$1/4$ teaspoon mustard seeds
Juice of $1/2$ a small lime
$1/2$ teaspoon ground fresh ginger
1 to 2 cloves garlic, finely sliced
2-inch stick cinnamon
5 black peppercorns
$1/2$ to 1 teaspoon maldive fish flakes
Salt to taste
Freshly milled black pepper to taste
1 cup grated coconut

Tomato Sambol

Serves 2 to 4

Char-grilled tomatoes are delicately perfumed and flavored with an array of complementary ingredients to yield this appetizing *sambol*.

Preheat the broiler. Cut the tomato in 2 and broil (cut side up) for a few minutes. Traditionally tomato is roasted and charred over hot coals. When ready the tomato should be slightly charred and still holding its shape. Let cool and rest for approximately 15 minutes.

Cut the tomato into small ($1/3$ to $1/2$-inch) pieces and place in a medium bowl. If desired peel the skin off before cutting.

Combine the oil, chili flakes, and garlic in a small nonstick pan. Season with salt and fry on moderately high heat for approximately 20 seconds, until the chili starts to brown and crisp. Stir constantly. Transfer this mixture to the tomatoes and mix well.

Add the onion, coconut milk, maldive fish, and green chili. Mix well and season with lime and adjust salt. Leave for 5 to 10 minutes for the flavors to unify. Best served immediately.

1 firm moderately large
   tomato
$1^1/2$ teaspoons coconut oil
   or olive oil
$1/2$ to $3/4$ teaspoon red
   chili flakes
1 large clove garlic,
   finely chopped
Salt to taste
1 small red onion,
   finely sliced
1 tablespoon thick coconut
   milk (see page 31)
$1/2$ to $3/4$ teaspoon maldive
   fish flakes, pounded
1 medium green chili,
   finely chopped
Fresh lime juice to taste

Crunchy Carrot Saladé

Originating in the luscious hill country of Sri Lanka, this delicious savory salad is a unique delight.

Sprinkle a pinch of salt over the chopped green chili, if using and leave for 2 to 3 minutes.

In a medium bowl combine the carrots, onion, coconut, curry leaves, lime, and green chili. Season with salt and pepper. Mix thoroughly to evenly distribute all the ingredients and flavors. Refrigerate until time to serve. (For best results, refrigerate for a minimum of 10 minutes.) This humble salad is at its best when served with rice.

Salt to taste
1 medium green chili, finely
    chopped (optional)
1 tightly packed cup roughly
    grated carrots (about 3
    medium carrots)
1/2 medium red onion,
    finely chopped
1 to 1 1/2 heaped teaspoons
    grated coconut
2 curry leaves, finely sliced
Fresh lime juice to taste
Freshly milled black pepper
    to taste

Gotukola Saladé

Gotukola is a variety of broad-leaf parsley that grows abundantly in Sri Lanka. This is a delicious salad that is quick and simple to prepare. The substitution of parsley for *gotukola* will not compromise the integrity of this gorgeous recipe.

Sprinkle a pinch of salt over the chopped green chilies and leave for 1 to 2 minutes.

In a medium bowl combine the *gotukola* leaves, onion, maldive fish, coconut, and green chili. Season with salt and pepper and plenty of lime juice. Mix thoroughly to evenly distribute all the ingredients and flavors.

Let rest for a few minutes for the bouquet of flavors to develop. Best served within 20 minutes at room temperature or slightly cooled in the refrigerator.

Salt to taste
1 medium green chili, finely
   chopped
1¾ tightly packed cups
   finely chopped *gotukola*
   leaves
½ medium red onion, finely
   chopped
½ to 1 teaspoon maldive
   fish flakes
1 to 1½ heaping teaspoons
   grated coconut
Freshly milled black pepper
   to taste
Fresh lime juice to taste

Sassy Egg Salad

While the heat in this side dish will complement an overall mild menu, the convergence of the ingredients will introduce a new element and depth of flavor to the meal.

Hard-boil the eggs in salted water; avoid overcooking them. For this recipe, the eggs are best with the yolks, cooked to a vibrant color and creamy texture. Peel and cut the eggs lengthwise into halves.

Sprinkle a pinch of salt on the chopped chilies and let them stand for 1 to 2 minutes. In a bowl combine the chilies, tomatoes, lime juice if using, and onion. Mix well and season with salt and pepper.

On a serving platter, arrange the egg halves with the yolk sides up and season with salt and pepper. Evenly sprinkle the tomato mixture over the eggs.

Variation
For an enjoyable variation that will give this recipe a new dimension, fry the whole eggs before cutting; see the variation for Yellow Rice (page 76).

6 large eggs
Salt to taste
1 to 3 medium green chilies, finely sliced
2 medium tomatoes, finely cubed
Fresh lime juice to taste (optional)
1 medium red onion, finely chopped
Freshly milled black pepper to taste

Lunu Miris

This fiery hot traditional recipe is essentially a combination of chili, maldive fish, and red onion. Exclusively for the most daring customer, *Lunu Miris* (salt chili) is served with most traditional staples.

In a medium bowl combine the onion, chili powder, chili flakes, and maldive fish. Mix and season with lime juice and salt.

Grind the above ingredients to a fairly smooth thick paste. Adjust salt and lime juice.

1 small red onion, finely chopped
2 tablespoons chili powder
$1/2$ teaspoon red chili flakes
1 teaspoon maldive fish flakes
Fresh lime juice to taste
Salt to taste

Katta Sambol

This red chili preparation is like dynamite and is served with most traditional staples. Here is a recipe that will add a definite zing to your meal.

Combine the onion, maldive fish, chili flakes, and chili powder in a mortar. Season with lime juice and salt. Pound and grind for a few minutes and adjust salt.

Katta Sambol is traditionally served with staples such as Milk Rice (page 74), *Pittu* (page 88), and Traditional Hoppers (page 91).

1 medium red onion, finely chopped
3 to 4 tablespoons maldive fish flakes
2 tablespoons red chili flakes
1 teaspoon chili powder
Fresh lime juice to taste
Salt to taste

Cool Cucumber Saladé

A cooling contrast to a fiery hot meal, this simple salad is an all-time Sri-Lankan favorite. It is best served over a bed of steamed rice.

Peel the cucumber and run the tines of a fork down the length of it. This will result in a decorative edge when the cucumber is sliced. Cut the cucumber into thin slices.

Sprinkle a pinch of salt over the green chilies and allow the chilies to rest for 2 to 3 minutes.

In a bowl combine the cucumber, green chilies, onion, lime juice if using, and coconut milk. Mix well, season to taste with salt and pepper, and chill in the refrigerator.

Variation
For a fun difference in flavor, either mix 1 tablespoon of plain yogurt with the coconut milk or substitute 2 tablespoons of plain yogurt for the coconut milk and combine with the remaining ingredients as described above.

1 large cucumber
Salt to taste
1 to 2 small green chilies, finely chopped
1/2 medium red onion, finely sliced
Fresh lime juice to taste (optional)
1/3 to 1/2 cup thick coconut milk (see page 31)
Freshly milled black pepper to taste

Cabbage Mallum

Serves 4 to 6

Tangy mustard adds a kick to this dreamy recipe while the delicate sweetness of coconut harmonizes with, and complements the earthy flavor of the cabbage.

Place the cabbage, onion, oil, and 1⅓ cups water in a small saucepan. Cook covered on medium heat for 8 to 10 minutes. For the success of this recipe, it is imperative that you do NOT add salt at this point.

Add the maldive fish if using, ground mustard, mustard seeds, coconut, green chili, curry leaves, ginger, garlic, peppercorns, turmeric powder, cumin seeds, and cinnamon to the pan. Cook, uncovered, on moderate heat for 6 to 8 minutes. Season with salt and pepper and stir frequently to prevent burning.

When ready, you will hear the mixture gently fry, the cabbage will be cooked and the coconut delicately roasted (not browned but to the point where the flavors are heightened). Cabbage Mallum is especially delightful served with red rice.

½ pound green cabbage, finely chopped (about 2⅔ cups)
1 small onion, finely chopped
2 to 3 teaspoons vegetable oil
½ teaspoon maldive fish flakes (optional)
¼ to ½ teaspoon ground mustard
⅛ teaspoon mustard seeds
1 to 1½ tablespoons grated coconut
1 medium green chili, finely chopped
5 curry leaves
½ teaspoon finely chopped fresh ginger
1 large clove garlic, finely chopped
6 black peppercorns
⅛ teaspoon turmeric powder
¼ teaspoon cumin seeds
2-inch stick cinnamon
Salt to taste
Freshly milled black pepper to taste

Seeni Sambol

The essence of *Seeni Sambol* is the contrasting flavors of sweet and spicy, which combine beautifully to complement the gently fried onions. This delightful onion dish is simply perfect when teamed with either Stringhoppers (page 89) or Milk Rice (page 74).

Heat the oil in a medium pan. Add the onions, curry leaves, sugar, chili powder, chili flakes, cloves, cardamoms, cinnamon, maldive fish, turmeric powder, and mustard seeds. Fry for approximately 1 minute on high heat and stir frequently.

Season with salt and add the tamarind juice if using. Cover and cook on moderately low heat for 8 to 10 minutes. Stir occasionally. Cover and shallow-fry on medium heat until the onions are cooked. Stir occasionally. When ready, the onions will have acquired a deep brown hue. *Seeni Sambol* can be either served warm or at room temperature.

Variation

A crispy version of *Seeni Sambol* can be prepared by deep-frying the onions (finely sliced) until golden brown and maldive fish (only dipped in the hot oil as overfrying will make it very tough). Use approximately 2 tablespoons maldive fish flakes (use slightly larger flakes). In a hot pan combine the fried onions and maldive fish with the remaining ingredients (excluding the tamarind juice) and cook for 30 to 40 seconds, stirring constantly. Add the tamarind juice and season with salt. This preparation can be preserved for a good three weeks by placing in an airtight container and refrigerating.

4 tablespoons vegetable oil
4 large red onions, finely chopped
6 to 8 curry leaves
1 1/2 to 2 teaspoons sugar
1 to 2 teaspoons chili powder
1 to 2 teaspoons red chili flakes
5 whole cloves
5 cardamom pods
2-inch stick cinnamon
3/4 to 1 teaspoon maldive fish flakes
1/8 to 1/4 teaspoon turmeric powder
1/2 teaspoon mustard seeds
Salt to taste
1 teaspoon tamarind juice (optional)

Mackerel Salad

Quick and simple to prepare, this fish salad is best complemented by white or red rice.

Drain the jack mackerel liquid and carefully clean the fish. Remove the bones and separate the fish fillets into fairly large pieces.

Sprinkle a pinch of salt over the sliced green chilies and leave for 1 to 2 minutes.

In a medium bowl combine the onion, tomato if using, and green chilies. Mix and season with lime juice, salt, and pepper.

Add the delicate fish and carefully mix. Adjust salt and pepper. Transfer to a serving dish. This salad can be served at room temperature or slightly cold.

1 (15-ounce) can jack mackerel
Salt to taste
1 to 3 medium green chilies, finely sliced
1 medium red onion, finely chopped
1 small firm tomato, chopped (optional)
Fresh lime juice to taste
Freshly milled black pepper to taste

Kale Mallum

Serves 4

Uncomplicated and demure, the persona of this entrée is one of extreme simplicity. This recipe will preserve the vibrant green color and inherent delicate flavor of the kale.

Heat the oil in a medium pan. Add the onion and green chili and fry on high heat for 30 to 40 seconds. Add the mustard seeds, turmeric powder, cumin seeds, and kale. Season with salt and pepper and cook on moderate heat for approximately 1 minute. Stir constantly.

Add 1 cup water and cover and cook on moderate heat for 10 to 12 minutes. Stir occasionally. Add the coconut and lime juice if using. Adjust salt, cover and cook for another 4 to 5 minutes. The kale will turn a brilliant green and the coconut a pale yellow.

This preparation is best served over steamed sticky white rice.

2 tablespoons vegetable oil
1 medium onion, finely chopped
1 large green chili, chopped
$1/8$ to $1/4$ teaspoon mustard seeds
Pinch to $1/8$ teaspoon turmeric powder
$1/4$ teaspoon cumin seeds
3 to $3^1/2$ cups tightly packed finely chopped kale leaves
Salt to taste
Freshly milled black pepper to taste
2 tablespoons grated coconut
Fresh lime juice to taste (optional)

RICE AND OTHER STAPLES

Rice is presented in many forms on our tables, varying from the simple
steamed daily version to the more elaborate fried, pilau, *buriyani*,
and other versions. Sri Lankan cuisine has a variety of other
diverse staples that supplement the primary food. The delicate Coconut Roti,
beautiful Stringhoppers, and exquisite Hoppers are just a few of the
unique fares that often grace our tables. These traditional staples
are eye-catching works of art and a guaranteed treat to the taste buds.

Milk Rice

Kiri Bath

Kiri Bath is a simple recipe that crosses all class and race barriers and is always a welcome treat. Especially appreciated as a weekend breakfast, this delicious traditional rice ensemble is always served on auspicious occasions.

In a medium saucepan, combine the rice with 3 cups water and season with salt. Bring to a boil, cover, and cook on low heat for approximately 6 minutes.

Add the coconut milk, cover, and simmer for 12 to 14 minutes. Adjust seasoning and cook, uncovered, on moderately high heat for 3 to 5 minutes (this allows the preparation to thicken). Stir continuously with a wooden spoon and gently mash the rice. When ready, the rice should be perfectly cooked, with a thick and creamy consistency.

2 cups rice
Salt to taste
3 cups coconut milk

Turn off the heat and allow the *Kiri Bath* to cool for a few minutes. Dish onto a flat serving dish and using the back of a spoon, smooth out to form an approximately 2-inch-high layer. With a knife gently score or cut into diamond shapes. Once cooled to room temperature, the cut rice can be carefully lifted out and re-plated.

Traditionally *Kiri Bath* is served with either *Lunu Miris* (page 65) or *Katta Sambol* (page 66). It is equally delicious served with a spicy fish or meat curry.

Variation
This version of *Kiri Bath* cannot be cut and lifted as pieces, but will have a loose and creamy consistency similar to that of porridge. This extremely delicious version for convenience is rarely served on special occasions. Cook the rice as described above, then add an extra 3/4 cup of coconut milk. Cook, uncovered, on high heat for another minute and stir constantly. Adjust salt.

Cilantro Rice

This wonderfully flavorful yet unpretentious rice preparation complements many Sri Lankan curry recipes. The fried cilantro leaves elevate this recipe in both flavor and fragrance.

Heat the oil and margarine (or use 2 tablespoons of ghee instead) in a medium saucepan. Add the coriander, garlic, ginger, onion, cumin seeds, peppercorns, cloves, and cardamoms. Fry for approximately 1½ minutes and stir constantly to prevent burning.

Add the rice and stir gently until every grain of rice is coated with the oil. Fry for 18 to 20 seconds. Add 4 cups water and season with salt to taste. Cover and cook on high until you see bubbles begin to break the water's surface. Immediately lower heat to moderately low, and cook covered for approximately 20 minutes. If using an open flame, it is advisable to use a heat dissipater to ensure the rice is cooked evenly.

When ready, the rice will have absorbed all the water and be cooked to perfection. It is imperative to the success of this recipe that the rice not be disturbed during cooking. Once cooked, take off the heat, remove the lid, and carefully fluff the rice with a spoon. Re-cover the rice using a clean, dry kitchen cloth for a minimum of 20 minutes. (This allows the excess moisture be absorbed by the cloth.)

While the rice is setting, cut the potato into approximately 1-inch cubes and deep-fry until golden brown and crisp. Season with a pinch of chili powder and salt to taste. Serve the rice and garnish with the fried potatoes.

1 tablespoon vegetable oil
1 tablespoon margarine or butter
1 cup finely chopped fresh cilantro leaves and young stalks
2 cloves garlic, finely chopped
1 tablespoon finely chopped fresh ginger
1 small red onion, finely sliced
¼ teaspoon cumin seeds
8 to 10 black peppercorns
6 whole cloves
6 cardamom pods
2 cups rice (basmati or sooduru samba)
Salt to taste
1 medium potato, peeled

Yellow Rice

Serves 4

This traditional yellow rice dish will bring the brilliance of the sun and the flavors of the earth to your table. The delectable coconut milk and aromatic ingredient infusion make this special rice recipe one to be savored.

In a medium saucepan heat the ghee. Add the onion, garlic, ginger, lemongrass, pandan leaf, curry leaves, cloves, cardamoms, and peppercorns. Fry for approximately 20 seconds and stir continuously to prevent burning.

Add the rice and stir to ensure each grain is coated with the oil. Pour in the coconut milk and 3 cups water. Season to taste with salt. Add the saffron or turmeric powder, cover, and cook on high heat until bubbles start to break the liquid surface. Immediately lower heat and cook, covered, on moderately low heat for approximately 20 minutes. When ready, the rice will be cooked to perfection and will have absorbed all the liquid. If using an open flame it is best to use a heat dissipater to guarantee the even cooking of the rice.

Take off the heat, remove the lid, and with a spoon, gently fluff the rice and mix in the raisins if using. Cover the rice with a clean, dry kitchen cloth and for best results leave for a minimum of 20 minutes.

Variation

For an extra dimension of flavor, add 4 hardboiled eggs that have been fried to a crispy golden brown as a delectable garnish. Peel the boiled eggs and with a sharp pin prick each egg all over the surface. (This helps prevent the eggs from bursting during frying.) Heat 2 to 3 tablespoons of vegetable oil and season with a pinch of turmeric powder and salt. Add the eggs and fry (stirring constantly) until beautifully colored and crispy textured. Cut the eggs lengthwise into halves and stud the dished rice.

$1^{1}/_{2}$ to 2 tablespoons ghee, melted
1 small red onion, finely sliced
3 cloves garlic, sliced
$^{1}/_{2}$ tablespoon finely chopped fresh ginger
4-inch stalk lemongrass
2-inch piece pandan leaf (*rampa*)
6 to 8 curry leaves
6 whole cloves
6 cardamom pods
8 to 10 black peppercorns
2 cups rice (muthu samba, sooduru samba or basmati)
1 cup coconut milk
Salt to taste
1 tablespoon saffron strands or $^{1}/_{2}$ to 1 teaspoon saffron powder or $^{1}/_{4}$ teaspoon turmeric powder
$^{1}/_{3}$ to $^{1}/_{2}$ cup raisins (optional)

Rice Pilau

This basic pilaf is enhanced by the flavors of chicken stock, bacon, onions, and heavenly fragrant spices. The beautiful raisins contribute a perfect touch of sweetness to this recipe, while the green peas enhance the aesthetics of the dish.

Heat the oil or ghee in a medium saucepan. Add the onion, curry leaves, peppercorns, cardamoms, cloves, garlic, and ginger. Fry for approximately 20 seconds and stir constantly to prevent burning. Add the rice and fry for another few seconds and stir to ensure the rice grains are completely coated with the oil.

Add the green peas and stock and season to taste with salt. Cover and cook on high heat until bubbles start to break the liquid surface. Immediately reduce heat and simmer, covered, on moderately low heat for approximately 20 minutes. Remember to use a heat dissipater if cooking on an open flame.

Take off heat, remove the lid, and gently fluff the rice with a spoon. Place a clean, dry kitchen cloth over the rice and leave for a minimum of 20 minutes. Carefully dish the rice onto a serving platter and garnish with the raisins and fried bacon if using.

1 tablespoon vegetable oil or ghee
1 small red onion, finely chopped
6 curry leaves
5 black peppercorns
4 cardamom pods
4 whole cloves
1 teaspoon ground garlic
1 teaspoon ground fresh ginger
2 cups basmati rice
1/2 cup thawed frozen green peas
4 cups mild chicken or vegetable stock
Salt to taste
1 tablespoon raisins
2 ounces bacon, cut into small pieces and fried until crispy (optional)

Tamarind Rice

Pulichatham

Serves 4 to 6

This beautiful traditional Tamil recipe is an absolute treat to the taste buds. Here is a melting pot with the unique flavors of tamarind, dill, and chickpeas blending to complement and enhance the overall preparation.

If using dry chickpeas, soak overnight and boil in salted water until tender.

Heat 1 tablespoon oil in a medium saucepan and add the rice. Fry for approximately 15 seconds and stir to ensure each grain of rice is coated with the oil. Add 4 cups water, cover, and cook on high until bubbles start breaking the surface. If using an open flame, it is best to use a heat dissipater to guarantee even cooking. Immediately reduce heat and cook, covered, on moderately low heat for approximately 20 minutes. Take off heat and gently fluff the rice and cover with a clean, dry kitchen cloth.

In a medium saucepan combine the remaining oil, onion, mustard seeds, dill, curry leaves, chilies, and butter. Season with salt and fry on moderately high heat until the onions are beautifully browned (20 to 30 seconds). Stir constantly to prevent burning. Add the tamarind solution and cook for 1 to 1 1/2 minutes on high heat. Adjust salt.

Stir in the cooked rice (if rice is very sticky, drizzle an extra tablespoon of vegetable oil over the rice) cover, and simmer on low heat for 12 to 15 minutes. Stir in the chickpeas and adjust salt. Take off heat and cover with a clean, dry kitchen cloth for 15 to 20 minutes. Alternatively, the rice can finish off in a preheated (350°F) oven. Fluff the rice occasionally.

1 cup chickpeas (canned or dry)
1 1/2 tablespoons vegetable oil
2 cups basmati rice
2 tablespoons vegetable oil or ghee
1 medium red onion, finely sliced
2 teaspoons mustard seeds
1/2 to 1 teaspoon dill seeds or 2 tablespoons chopped dill leaves
8 curry leaves
8 to 10 whole dry red chilies (medium or large)
Salt to taste
3 to 4 tablespoons margarine or butter
2 teaspoons (or to taste) tamarind paste stirred into 3/4 cup water

Steamed Rice

Steamed Rice, also known as Boiled Rice and Plain Rice, is the healthiest and simplest form of rice preparation. Very often served for lunch in Sri Lanka, this versatile preparation can accompany a multitude of curries and salads.

In a medium saucepan, combine the rice with 4 cups water. Keep in mind that sooduru and muthu samba require slightly less water and that red rice requires a little extra. Bring to a boil and season with salt. Cover and simmer on moderately low heat for approximately 20 minutes. It is best to use a heat dissipater if cooking on an open flame, as it ensures even cooking.

2 cups rice (basmati, sooduru samba, muthu samba, samba, or red)
Pinch of salt

Alternatively, steamed rice is effortlessly prepared in a rice cooker.

Variation

This method, if followed through, guarantees each grain of rice will be cooked to fluffy perfection. Further, it eliminates some of the undesirable starch.

Bring a large pot of water to a rolling boil and season with the salt.

In the meantime, wash 2 cups of basmati rice in warm water and soak the washed rice in warm water for precisely 10 minutes. Drain the rice, add it to the boiling water, and cook for 10 to 12 minutes. Test the rice for doneness by rubbing a few grains between your fingers. The rice should be cooked through the center when done.

Have a large strainer ready in your sink and pour in the boiled rice. Rinse the rice with plenty of hot water. Reheat the rice prior to serving.

Lamb Buriyani

Serves 4

*B*uriyani is a very popular, tremendously delicious rice dish with its preparation initially perfected by the Muslim community. This rice is often served at special functions and festive occasions. It is also good with mutton or chicken instead of lamb.

For the curry, heat the oil in a small saucepan and fry the onion until golden brown. Add the turmeric powder, cumin seeds, garlic, ginger, chili powder, paprika powder if using, crushed pepper, peppercorns, cloves, cardamoms, and cinnamon. Fry for 8 to 10 seconds and season with salt and pepper. Stir constantly to prevent burning.

Add the meat and, stirring constantly, cook on high heat for approximately 3 minutes. Adjust salt and cook for another 10 seconds. Add $2/3$ cup water, bring to a boil, adjust salt to taste, cover, and simmer on low heat for approximately 20 minutes. Stir in the yogurt, cover, and simmer for another 10 minutes. To thicken the gravy, cook, uncovered, on high heat (stirring continuously) for 4 to 6 minutes.

While the curry is cooking make the rice. Heat the oil in a medium saucepan. Add the rice and stir to coat each grain with oil. Season to taste with salt and pepper. Add the stock together with 2 cups water, cover, and cook on high heat until bubbles begin to break the surface. Immediately reduce heat, cover, and simmer on moderately low heat for approximately 20 minutes. (If using an open flame, it is best to use a heat dissipater to ensure even cooking.) Remove lid, take off heat, and sprinkle in the food colorings. (Liquid food coloring can be used instead of powder. To use, dilute 1 to 2 drops of the coloring in approximately $3/4$ teaspoon water.) Leave for 40 to 50 seconds and gently fluff the rice with a spoon. Cover with a clean, dry kitchen cloth and leave until the curry is cooked.

FOR THE CURRY

2 tablespoons vegetable oil
1 small onion, finely sliced
$1/2$ teaspoon turmeric powder
$1/4$ teaspoon cumin seeds
3 large cloves garlic, finely chopped
1 tablespoon finely chopped fresh ginger
1 teaspoon chili powder
$1/2$ to 1 teaspoon paprika powder (optional)
$1/4$ to $1/2$ teaspoon crushed black pepper
8 black peppercorns
6 whole cloves
6 cardamom pods
2-inch stick cinnamon
Salt to taste
Freshly milled black pepper to taste
$1 1/2$ pounds lamb, cut into approximately $1 1/2$-inch pieces (include a few pieces with a few bones)
2 to 3 tablespoons natural yogurt

Once the curry is ready, uncover the rice and with a spoon carefully make deep pockets in the rice and fill these with the meat and gravy. Cover the stuffed pockets with rice. Sprinkle the drops of rose essence over the preparation and evenly distribute the green chilies if using. Cover the saucepan and cook evenly (use a heat dissipater if necessary) on very low heat for heat 15 to 20 minutes.

While the rice is cooking, deep-fry the onion until golden brown and crispy. Drain on absorbent paper and season with salt.

Carefully spoon the *Buriyani* on to a serving plate. When plating, the meat pieces will intermingle with the colored and white grains of rice. Garnish with the fried onions.

Variation

For a flavorful difference, substitute 8 medium tiger prawns (heads removed) for ½ pound of the meat. This mixed version is a true masterpiece.

FOR THE RICE

1 to 2 tablespoons vegetable oil
2 cups basmati rice
Salt to taste
Freshly milled black pepper to taste
2 cups mild mutton stock or water
Pinch orange food color powder or few drops of liquid food color
Pinch yellow food color powder or few drops of liquid food color
Few drops rose essence or 1 to 2 teaspoons rose water
6 small green chilies (optional)
1 medium onion, finely sliced

Fragrant Fried Rice

Serves 4

The rice is discretely flavored and perfumed with butter, vegetables, and aromatic spices while the shrimp wonderfully complements the overall recipe.

Heat the butter and vegetable oil in a medium skillet. Add the shrimp if using, leeks, carrots, curry leaves, peppercorns, cloves, cardamoms, cinnamon, and turmeric powder. Season with salt and pepper and cook on moderately high heat for 2 to 3 minutes. Stir constantly to prevent burning.

Add the rice and mix well to distribute all the ingredients. Cook on moderate heat for 1 to 2 minutes and adjust salt and pepper. Stir frequently and ensure each grain of rice is delicately fried.

Variation

To further enhance flavor and texture, stir 2 large eggs that have been scrambled into the above fried rice.

2 to 3 tablespoons butter or margarine
1 teaspoon vegetable oil
15 to 20 small shrimp, shelled (optional)
1 cup julienned leeks
1 cup julienned carrots
3 to 4 curry leaves
8 black peppercorns
3 to 5 whole cloves
3 to 5 cardamom pods
2-inch stick cinnamon
Pinch of turmeric powder
Salt to taste
Freshly milled coarse black pepper to taste
6 to 7 cups cooked white rice (muthu, sooduru samba, or basmati)

Savory Coconut Roti

Pol Roti   *Makes 6 (4-inch) roti*

An all-time favorite, this amazingly simple and extremely delicious traditional flat bread makes a unique breakfast and enjoyable dinner entrée. The delicate flavor and intriguing texture of the coconut make this flat bread a unique treat.

In a medium bowl combine the flour and coconut. Mix well and season with salt.

Gradually add 3 to 4 tablespoons of water and mix to form a dough. Do not overwork the dough. Divide the dough into 6 and shape them into separate rounds. On a lightly floured surface, roll out the rounds to form approximately 4-inch-wide discs. Alternatively, you could roll out the dough on a lightly floured surface and cut out the discs using a pastry cutter, or an inverted cup or bowl.

2 cups flour
$1/3$ to $1/2$ cup grated coconut
Salt to taste

Heat a flat nonstick pan. Lightly grease with oil and cook the *roti* on moderately high heat for approximately 3 minutes per side. Ideally, Coconut Roti should be crisp and golden brown on the outside and soft and cooked through in the center.

Coconut Roti is delicious served with *Katta Sambol* (page 66) and/or a spicy meat or fish curry with a dollop of butter on the side. Coconut Roti make a fun breakfast or snack when served with butter and jam.

Uppu Ma

Cashew nuts, curry leaves, red chili, mustard seeds, and onion introduce layers of flavor and texture to this semolina-based dish. This traditional Tamil breakfast recipe also makes a welcome teatime snack.

Combine the ghee and cashews in a small non-stick saucepan. Cook on moderately high heat and fry until golden brown. Stir frequently to prevent burning. Lift out the nuts and drain the excess oil on absorbent paper. Set aside.

Take the saucepan off the heat and add the chilies, onion, and curry leave to the remaining hot ghee. Return to heat and cook on high for 30 to 40 seconds. Stir constantly. Add the mustard seeds and fry for another 5 seconds. Stir in the semolina and fry on moderately high heat for 2 to 3 minutes, until golden brown. Stir frequently to prevent burning.

Add the turmeric powder, milk, season with salt, and simmer on low heat until all the liquid has been absorbed and the semolina cooked (30 to 40 seconds). If very thick add $1/8$ to $1/4$ cup water. Stir constantly. Take off the heat, adjust salt, and stir in the cashews. Gently fluff with a fork and serve while warm. Traditionally buttermilk is used in this recipe.

1 to $1^1/4$ tablespoons ghee
6 to 8 cashew nuts, roughly chopped
2 to 3 whole dry red chilies, broken into $1/2$-inch pieces
1 small red onion, finely sliced
8 to 10 small curry leaves
1 teaspoon mustard seeds
$1/2$ cup semolina
Pinch of turmeric powder
1 cup 2% milk
Salt to taste

Variation

Traditional *Uppu Ma* has a more porridge-like consistency. This can easily be achieved by increasing the quantity of milk by $1/3$ to $1/2$ cup.

Buttermilk, with its distinct mildly tart flavor (similar to plain yogurt), is used in the authentic preparation of *Uppu Ma*. Simply substitute buttermilk (preferably the reduced fat kind) for the 2% milk.

Idly

Serves 4

Idly is a traditional Tamil entrée that is steamed until cooked and acquires a light and spongy consistency. This typical breakfast dish is ideal for dinner or lunch and is especially delicious when served with a spicy traditional curry. *Idly* molds are available in Indian grocery stores.

Soak the urad dhal for 4 hours. Drain and puree.

In a large bowl combine the urad dhal puree, semolina, and 1½ to 1⅔ cups water. Mix well, cover, and leave in a warm place until the batter rises and approximately doubles in volume. This process will take 12 to 24 hours depending on the season. Just before making the *idly*, season with salt.

1 cup split urad dhal
1½ cups steamed coarse
 semolina (page 23)
Salt to taste
Butter

Grease the *idly* molds with butter and fill each mold with the thick airy batter. Place the mold rack in a steamer (large pan with water at the bottom), cover, and cook for approximately 15 minutes, until cooked through. Replenish as necessary with boiling water. The cooked *idly* should come off the molds effortlessly. Repeat the above process until all the batter is transformed into the delicious staple. *Idly* is traditionally served with *Sambar* and Coconut Sambol (page 58).

Tip
Sambar is a beautiful soupy curry based on vegetables and dhals. It has a distinct flavor and is traditionally served with *idly* and *thosai*. *Sambar* spice mixes are readily available in Asian markets. Simply follow the packet instructions and add the vegetables you love. This curry is especially delicious with a zucchini, eggplant, potato, green peppers, and tomatoes.

Traditional Thosai

Serves 4 to 6

The South Indian influence on Sri Lankan cuisine is evident in this recipe, which has been treasured and perfected by the Tamil community of Sri Lanka. These delicious lace-like savory flat breads are an absolutely mouthwatering delight.

Soak the urad dhal for about 4 hours, drain and puree. In a large bowl combine the urad dhal puree, all-purpose flour, and rice flour together with 1½ cups water. Mix well to ensure even distribution of all the ingredients. Cover and leave in a warm place until the batter rises and approximately doubles in volume. This process will take 12 to 24 hours depending on the season.

Thin the risen batter by adding 1½ cups water and when ready to make the *thosai*, season with salt. The unseasoned batter can be covered and refrigerated about 1 day. Heat a medium flat pan (preferably nonstick). Lightly grease the surface of the pan with oil or spray. Ladle about ⅓ cup of the batter and (with the back of a spoon) starting in the center and moving out in a circular pattern spread to evenly coat the base of the pan with the batter to make an 8 to 9-inch *thosai*.

1 cup split urad dhal
1 cup steamed all-purpose flour (page 23)
½ cup steamed white rice flour (page 23)
Salt to taste
Vegetable oil (optionally seasoned with sesame oil)

Cook on moderate heat until the bottom of the *thosai* turns golden. This should occur within 40 to 50 seconds. Turn the *thosai* over and cook for another few seconds. The cooked *thosai* will have a lacy and airy quality about it. Regrease the pan and continue in a similar fashion to make *thosai* with all of the batter.

Variations

For a quick and simpler version, soak 1 cup urad dhal and 2 cups basmati rice (you can use other types too) for about 2 hours in slightly warm water. In a small bowl, combine 2 cups warm water, 1 teaspoon yeast, and 2 teaspoons sugar. Mix well and set aside for about 5 minutes. Place this mixture in a blender with the urad dhal and the rice. Blend to form a smooth batter. Transfer to a large bowl, cover, and let rise in a warm place until approximately doubles in volume (about 1½ hours). Dilute with 2½ to 3 cups water, season with salt, and make the *thosai* as above. As described below, a fried onion mixture also can be added to this batter.

Finely slice a medium red onion and fry until golden brown in a tablespoon of vegetable oil. Add 5 to 6 whole dry chilies that have been broken into approximately ¾-inch pieces, 10 to 15 small curry leaves, and 2 to 3 medium green chilies (chopped). Fry for another 20 seconds and season with salt. Stir constantly. Stir in the mixture to the seasoned batter and make the *thosai* as described above.

Alternatively, have at hand a finely chopped red onion, a few curry leaves, and 2 to 3 finely chopped green chilies and sprinkle a bit of this (unfried) mixture over each poured and spread *thosai*.

Masala Thosai is a delicious variation in which the Traditional Thosai is filled with a portion of the spiced potato mixture used for *Ala Bola* (page 41).

Pittu

Pittu is a wonderfully flavorful blend of coconut and rice flour that is steamed to perfection. This preparation is typically served as a breakfast or dinner item.

In a medium bowl combine the rice flour and salt. Mix to evenly distribute the salt and then add the water. With a spoon mix thoroughly for about 1 minute, transfer onto a flat surface and with your hands gently bring together. Using a pastry blender or an empty tin can with both its bases cut out, cut into the paste to break it up into ¼ to ½-inch pieces. These small pieces will resemble tiny balls and will be crumbly. Alternatively, the paste can be placed in a food processor and pulsed for a few seconds. For this method, if the paste is too wet it will clump into a ball. In this case simple add about a teaspoon of rice flour and then pulse.

2 cups steamed rice flour (steamed for an hour or lightly pan-roasted. Either white, red, or a combination of the two rice flours can be used; page 23)
¾ to 1 teaspoon salt
2 cups boiling water
3 to 6 tablespoons grated coconut

(The conventional method, recommended only for the more experienced, is to form the tiny balls by breaking off small pieces of the mixture with the fingers and then in a circular motion rolling the piece between the fingers.)

Add the coconut to the above mixture. Mix carefully so as to evenly distribute the coconut and adjust salt to taste. Steam this mixture in a covered steamer for about 15 minutes. (During steaming ensure that the water does not run out.)

If using the traditional cylindrical *pittu* mold, fill the mold (to the brim) with the above mixture. Fit the cylinder securely to the accompanying pot (filled with water). Place the apparatus on the stove and when the steam begins to escape from the top, cover with the lid or with aluminum foil and steam until cooked, about 15 minutes. When ready, carefully take the cylindrical piece off the pot and, using a spoon handle, gently push the *pittu* (from the bottom) onto a dish. Repeat this filling and steaming process until all the mixture is made into *pittu*.

The traditional *pittu* apparatus will yield very presentable pieces where as the more modern method will yield an equally delicious but loose form of *pittu*. Traditionally, *pittu* is served with *Katta Sambol* (page 66), a spicy meat or fish curry, and coconut milk. In northern Sri Lanka, this staple is savored with ripe mango or banana.

Stringhoppers

Makes 25 to 30 (4-inch) stringhoppers

Stringhoppers will be a true delight for those who love noodles, rice sticks, or pasta. A unique offering, this dish is a healthful main course that is commonly served at breakfast and is a popular dinner staple. You can purchase or order stringhopper molds in Sri Lankan grocery stores.

In a medium bowl combine the flour and season with salt to taste. Gradually add the water and mix well to form an extremely smooth paste. (The amount of water required may slightly vary based on the variety of rice used to make the flour, how well steamed or roasted the flour is, and discrepancies in measuring the flour.) Keep the bowl covered, as the paste is easier to work with when warm. Lightly grease the surfaces (could use either the inner or outer, I recommend the inner as it holds the stringhopper mixture better) of the stringhopper molds with vegetable oil. Fit the disc with the tiniest perforations on the stringhopper apparatus and fill with the above paste.

2 cups steamed rice flour (steamed for an hour and sifted or lightly pan-roasted. Either white, red or a combination of white and red; page 23)
Salt to taste
2^1/$_2$ to 2^2/$_3$ cups boiling water
Vegetable oil

Hold the apparatus approximately an inch above the greased molds (one at a time) and pour the paste out of the apparatus into (or onto) the molds. The paste should come out in the form of continuous strands. (If the strands are breaking in midstream, the paste is too dry. Add a few drops of boiling water to remedy this.) Carefully pour the paste in a circular motion, to make approximately 2 layers. Ensure the surfaces of the molds are well covered with the mixture.

Form small stacks of 3 to 4 molds, place in a steamer, cover, and steam for approximately 6 minutes, until cooked. After the first batch is cooked remove the molds and carefully peel the stringhoppers off and place in a serving dish. Repeat the filling, greasing, pouring, and steaming processes until all the paste is used.

Variation
Substitute all-purpose flour (steamed for an hour and sifted) for ^{1}/$_2$ the quantity of the rice flour and you will have stringhoppers with a difference. These stringhoppers are generally thicker, slightly heavier, and more substantial than their rice flour counterpart.

Stringhopper Pilau

This delicious dish is honestly a meal in itself. Stringhopper Pilau is often served at special occasions and is fit for kings.

In a medium saucepan combine the chicken, stock, cardamoms, cloves, pepper, garlic, ginger, curry leaves, 1/2 teaspoon turmeric powder, chili powder, lime juice, and 7 to 8 cups water. Bring to a boil and season to taste with salt. Cover and simmer on moderately low heat for 35 to 45 minutes.

Transfer the chicken pieces to a medium bowl and mix in the remaining 1/2 teaspoon turmeric powder and season to taste with salt and pepper. Using the fingers, rub the seasoning onto the chicken.

Heat 6 tablespoons ghee or oil in a medium nonstick pan and add the chicken pieces. Fry on moderately high heat for 3 to 4 minutes and brown the chicken pieces. Remove the chicken pieces and drain on absorbent paper. With a sharp pin, prick the eggs all over the surfaces to prevent bursting during frying. Rub onto the eggs a pinch of turmeric powder and salt. Add to the hot oil in the chicken pan and fry for 2 to 3 minutes. Stir continuously until golden brown in hue and crispy in texture. Drain the excess oil on absorbent paper and cut lengthwise into halves.

Heat the remaining 6 tablespoons ghee in a large saucepan and add onion, green chilies, curry leaves, peppercorns, and fry for 40 to 50 seconds. Add the stringhopper pieces, Season to taste with salt and fry on high heat for 4 to 5 minutes. Stir carefully and constantly. Add the cooked chicken pieces to the stringhopper fry and mix with care to evenly distribute the pieces. Embed the egg halves (cut side down) in the pilau once it has been dished onto a serving platter.

8 skinless chicken parts
1 cup mild chicken stock
5 cardamom pods
5 whole cloves
1 teaspoon freshly milled coarse black pepper
4 large cloves garlic, finely chopped
1 tablespoon finely chopped fresh ginger
6 curry leaves
1 teaspoon turmeric powder
1/4 to 1/2 teaspoon chili powder
Few drops of fresh lime juice
Salt to taste
6 tablespoons ghee or vegetable oil
4 small eggs, hard boiled and peeled
6 tablespoons ghee
1 medium red onion, finely sliced
4 medium green chilies, chopped
8 curry leaves
6 to 8 black peppercorns
50 to 60 rice flour stringhoppers, broken into small pieces (page 89)

Traditional Hoppers

The crispy golden edge of this beautiful wok-shaped coconut-flavored crepe contrasts perfectly with its soft and spongy center. The flavor of a piece of crispy edge that you've dipped into the yolk of an egg hopper is simply heavenly.

Soak the rice in water for approximately 2½ hours. In a small bowl, combine the yeast, sugar and water (if the water is hot and not warm, it will kill the yeast). Mix well and set aside for a few minutes. Drain the rice and transfer to an electric blender. Add the coconut milks and blend for a few minutes to form a smooth batter. Transfer this batter to a large bowl and mix in the yeast mixture. Cover the bowl and leave in a warm place for 2 to 3 hours and let the batter rise until it approximately doubles in volume.

2⅔ cups raw white rice
1 leveled teaspoon active
   dry yeast
2 teaspoon sugar
½ cup warm water
2 cups thick coconut milk,
   room temperature
   (see page 31)
1 cup coconut milk
Salt to taste
⅓ to ½ cup vegetable oil

Just prior to making the hoppers, season the batter with salt. The unseasoned batter can be covered and kept refrigerated for about 1 day. You will need an open flame and a small wok (dedicated to making hoppers) with a lid. Have ready a small piece of cotton cloth that you can role up and dip in the oil. Heat the wok and apply the oil to cover the entire inner surface of the wok. Once the wok is smoking hot, take it off the flame and add a large spoon of the batter. Rotate the wok to swirl the batter right up to the brim and there should be enough batter in the pan to form a small hump at the base of the wok.

Return to the stove, cover, and cook on moderate heat for 2 to 3 minutes. Using a metal spatula, tease the hopper (which should have taken the shape of the wok) out of the wok and continue with the greasing of the wok, pouring in the batter, swirling, covering, and cooking until all the hoppers are made.

Variation on page 92

Variation
Egg hoppers are traditionally served alongside the plain hoppers. To make egg hoppers, simply break an egg into the base of the swirled batter, cover, and cook on moderately low heat until the egg is cooked. Season the egg with salt and pepper. It is best if the egg white is cooked through but the yolk still slightly creamy and runny.

Tip
If having difficulty removing the hoppers, mix a beaten egg yolk with the oil and then grease the hot wok by applying and rubbing it in.

Godamba Roti

Makes 8

Godamba Roti are delicious, paper-thin flat breads that are guaranteed to impress and delight. This simple staple is best served with a spicy Mutton Curry (page 141).

In a medium bowl combine the flour and salt. Mix to evenly distribute the salt. Gradually stir in $2/3$ to 1 cup of water. Mix to form the dough and knead for 40 to 50 seconds (avoid over-working the dough). If the dough is too sticky, sprinkle in a bit of flour. Divide into 8 equal portions and form each portion into a ball.

Pour the oil into a flat-based deep dish and place the dough balls in the oil. They should be entirely immersed in oil. Cover and leave for approximately 2 hours. (If not entirely immersed, either pour a little extra oil to top them off or carefully roll the dough balls in the oil and occasionally turn them over.)

2 cups all-purpose flour
$3/4$ teaspoon salt
2 to 3 cups vegetable oil

Heat a large nonstick pan. On a clean, flat surface, using the fingertips, stretch each dough ball into a paper-thin square or circular shape. (Expert *Godamba Roti* makers toss the dough in a way similar to the way pizza dough is tossed.) Transfer to the pan and cook on moderately low heat for approximately 1 minute per side until cooked. *Godamba Roti* are best served warm.

Variation

Egg Godamba Roti are extremely delicious and simply a breeze to prepare. Beat one small egg per *roti* and once the first side of a plain *Godamba Roti* begins to cook (on moderately low heat), carefully pour in the beaten egg making sure to evenly spread it over the *roti* center. Fold the four sides in and once the egg begins to set turn the *roti* over and cook for another 1 to 2 minutes. Traditionally, Egg Godamba Roti are served alongside plain *Godamba Roti*.

Chicken Koththu Roti

Serves 4 to 6

*K*oththu Roti is a beautiful concoction of chopped *Godamba Roti*, cabbage, and onion tied together by the delicious flavors of a classic *Koththu Roti* meat curry. This all-time favorite is absolutely a meal in itself.

Preheat the oven to 400°F. Remove the neck and giblets from the chicken body cavity. Rinse and pat dry. In a small bowl combine the turmeric powder, curry powder, coriander powder, garlic, ginger, pepper, and chili powder with 1 teaspoon of water. Mix together and season to taste with salt.

Generously rub the body and neck cavities of the chicken and sprinkle the skin with salt. Place the chicken, breast side up on a shallow roasting pan. Loosen the skin (it is best to use your fingers) and spread the spice mixture over the meat of the breasts and legs and the body cavity. Put the cloves, cardamoms, cinnamon stick, peppercorns, and 3 curry leaves into the body cavity. Brush the melted butter over the chicken breasts and legs.

Roast the chicken for approximately 50 minutes. Remove the chicken to a platter and let stand for 8 to 10 minutes. Transfer the oil and flavorful bits in the roasting tray and juices trapped in the body cavity into a small glass bowl. Let it settle, and carefully spoon out and discard some of the oil (which will float to the surface). Pour the rest into a small saucepan. Add the coconut milk and chili powder. Season with salt and cook on moderately high heat for 1 to 2 minutes. Stir constantly. Cut the chicken into 8 pieces (alternatively, take the meat off the bones and cut into bite-size pieces) and pour the gravy over the pieces.

Heat the oil in a large (preferably nonstick) skillet. Add the remaining 5 curry leaves, cabbage, onion, and green chilies. Cook on moderately high heat for 50 to 60 seconds and stir constantly. Mix in the *Godamba Roti* pieces, chili flakes, and season with salt and pepper. Stirring constantly cook for another 2 to 3 minutes. Make a little well in the mixture, add the beaten eggs (season with salt and pepper) and cook for another minute. Stir the egg mixture constantly (to scramble it) in a circular motion and gradually incorporate it into the *Koththu Roti* mixture. Ensure the egg is evenly distributed. Add the chicken (with its gravy), cook for another 1 to 2 minutes and adjust salt. Serve immediately.

1 medium whole chicken, 2 to 2 1/4 pounds
1/8 teaspoon turmeric powder
1/2 teaspoon roasted Sinhala curry powder
1 teaspoon coriander powder
4 cloves garlic, ground to a paste
1/2 to 3/4 teaspoon ginger powder
1/2 to 3/4 teaspoon freshly milled black pepper
1 teaspoon chili powder
Salt to taste
5 whole cloves
5 cardamom pods
2-inch stick cinnamon
6 black peppercorns
8 curry leaves
1 1/2 tablespoons butter, melted
1/3 cup thick coconut milk (see page 31)
1/2 teaspoon chili powder
2 1/2 to 3 1/2 tablespoons vegetable oil
1 to 1 1/2 cups finely sliced cabbage
2 medium onions, chopped
6 to 8 medium green chilies, chopped
8 *Godamba Roti*, chopped (page 93)
3/4 teaspoon red chili flakes
Freshly milled black pepper to taste
2 medium eggs, beaten

VEGETABLES

Since a wide variety of tropical vegetables are readily available to the cook,
the possibilities are a blank canvas and the ensuing recipes are
both promising and intriguing. Preserving the integrity and essence of
the vegetable itself is key to the success of these delicious recipes.
Therefore, vegetarian entrées are often mild with blends of exotic spices used
to enhance and complement the inherent flavors, textures, and hues.
In Sri Lankan cuisine, daily vegetarian preparations like Dhal Curry,
Ala Theldala, and Ash Plantain Curry are kept simple, while special dishes
such as Eggplant Moju and Cashews with Green Peas and Carrots are
more elaborate and complex.

Eggplant Moju

Serves 4 to 5

Enhanced by a perfect blend of spices and a hint of coconut milk, this classic eggplant preparation is guaranteed to appease the toughest customer.

Cut the eggplants into approximately 2 by $1/2$-inch fingers. Heat the oil in a medium pan and deep-fry the eggplant in batches. When ready, the eggplant should be a gorgeous golden brown hue and fairly crisp. Make sure to drain the excess oil on plenty of absorbent paper.

In a medium skillet combine the fried eggplant with the onion, garlic, ginger, mustard paste, green chilies, chili flakes, chili powder, turmeric powder, mustard seeds, and maldive fish if using. Season with salt and pepper. Cook for approximately 2 minutes on high heat and stir frequently to prevent burning. Adjust salt.

Add the coconut milk if using and cook for another 40 to 50 seconds. You will find that the coconut milk not only adds flavor to the recipe but also deglazes the pan and thus ensures that none of the tremendous flavors is lost. Mix in the lime juice and adjust salt.

Variation
For an interesting variation, add 10 to 12 deep-fried anchovy *karavala* (remove heads before frying).

2 medium eggplants ($1^1/2$ to 2 pounds total)
Oil for deep-frying
1 to $1^1/2$ medium red onions, finely chopped
6 large cloves garlic, ground to a paste
$2/3$ to 1 tablespoon finely chopped fresh ginger
1 teaspoon mustard paste
3 to 4 medium green chilies, sliced lengthwise in half but joined at the stem end
1 teaspoon red chili flakes
$1/2$ teaspoon red chili powder
$1/8$ teaspoon turmeric powder
$1/4$ teaspoon mustard seeds
$1/2$ to 1 teaspoon maldive fish flakes (optional)
Salt to taste
Freshly milled black pepper to taste
3 tablespoons coconut milk (optional)
Plenty of fresh lime juice to taste

Spicy Pineapple Sauté

Serves 4

This stir-fry is delightfully reminiscent of the tropical isle of Sri Lanka. The refreshing taste and aroma of the pineapple is enhanced by the intermingling flavors of exotic spices and luscious coconut milk.

Cut the pineapple into approximately ¾-inch pieces. If using the canned pineapple, drain well prior to incorporating in this recipe.

Heat the oil in a medium pan. Add the onion, mustard seeds, chili flakes, chili powder, curry leaves, turmeric powder, cloves, cardamoms, and cinnamon. Fry for approximately 30 seconds and stir constantly to prevent burning.

Add the pineapple pieces and season to taste with salt and pepper. Cook on moderately high heat for 2 to 3 minutes. Stir frequently.

Add the coconut milk, and cook for another 3 to 4 minutes on moderately high heat. Stir frequently and adjust salt and pepper. When ready, you will see the preparation come together. Turn the heat off, and let the preparation stand for 4 to 5 minutes before serving. Best served over a beautiful bed of Yellow Rice (page 76).

1 pound fresh or canned pineapple (10 slices)
2 tablespoons vegetable oil
1 medium red onion, finely chopped
⅛ to ¼ teaspoon mustard seeds
½ to ¾ teaspoon red chili flakes
⅛ teaspoon chili powder
3 curry leaves
¼ teaspoon turmeric powder
3 whole cloves
3 cardamom pods
2-inch stick cinnamon
Salt to taste
Freshly milled black pepper to taste
½ cup coconut milk

Beetroot Curry

Wonderfully colorful and delicately sweet, this beetroot curry is every child's delight and makes an ideal introduction to the adventure and diversity of the curry world.

Boil the beetroots in salted water; peel and cut (or grate) into small pieces.

Heat the oil in a medium pan. Add the onion, green chilies, mustard seeds, turmeric powder, coriander powder if using, curry leaves, and cinnamon if using. Fry for approximately 30 seconds and stir frequently to prevent burning.

Add the cooked beetroot and chili powder. Stirring frequently, cook on moderate heat for 4 to 5 minutes. Season to taste with salt and pepper. Stir in the mustard paste and coconut milk. Cook for another 2 to 3 minutes and adjust salt. The final consistency of the dish should be moist but not watery. This colorful beetroot preparation is best served with steamed white rice.

Variation
For an alternate method, instead of boiling the beetroots, peel, cut, and add them raw to the saucepan with the fried ingredients. Combine 1½ to 2 cups water, chili powder, mustard paste, and the coconut milk, cover, and simmer on moderate heat until the beetroot is cooked through and the final consistency achieved.

2 large beetroots
2 tablespoons vegetable oil
1 medium onion, finely chopped
1 to 2 medium green chilies, sliced
⅛ to ¼ teaspoon mustard seeds
⅛ to ¼ teaspoon turmeric powder
⅛ teaspoon coriander powder (optional)
4 to 6 curry leaves
2-inch stick cinnamon (optional)
¼ teaspoon chili powder
Salt to taste
Freshly milled black pepper to taste
¼ teaspoon mustard paste
4 to 6 tablespoons coconut milk

Cashews with Green Peas and Carrots

Luxuriously rich and divine, this traditional cashew preparation was and still is a symbol of high social standing. The green peas and carrots add a touch of gorgeous color to this mouthwatering recipe.

For best results soak the cashews in warm water for a minimum of 24 hours. Drain and replace the water 2 to 3 times during this period. Separate the whole cashew kernels into halves and drain the water.

Heat the oil in a medium saucepan. Add the mustard seeds, turmeric powder, chili powder, green chilies, curry leaves, fenugreek seeds, maldive fish, dill seeds if using, curry powder if using, and cinnamon. Fry on moderately high heat for 20 to 30 seconds. Stir constantly to prevent burning.

Add the cashews and season with salt. Cook for approximately 1 minute and stir frequently. Stir in the mustard paste, coconut milk, and $3/4$ cup water. Bring to a boil and adjust salt. Cover and cook on moderate heat for 30 minutes. Add the green peas and carrots and cook for approximately another 25 minutes.

Stir occasionally, being careful with the delicate cashew kernels. Ensure that the cashew is cooked through and watch for a moist but nonwatery consistency. (Add a little water if necessary.) This will be your indication that the preparation is ready. Traditionally, this recipe does not include green peas and carrots in its preparation.

$3/4$ pound (about 2 cups) raw cashew kernels
1 to $1^1/2$ tablespoons vegetable oil
$1/2$ medium red onion, finely chopped
1 teaspoon mustard seeds
$1/4$ teaspoon turmeric powder
$1/4$ to $1/2$ teaspoon chili powder
3 medium green chilies
8 curry leaves
$1/4$ teaspoon fenugreek seeds
$3/4$ to 1 tablespoon maldive fish flakes
$1/8$ teaspoon dill seeds (optional)
$1/2$ to 1 teaspoon raw Sinhala curry powder
2-inch stick cinnamon
Salt to taste
$1/2$ to 1 teaspoon mustard paste
3 cups coconut milk
1 cup frozen green peas and carrots

Okra Theldala

A definite favorite of mine, this recipe has none of the slimy mess normally associated with okra. In this delicious stir-fry, the onions, chili, and lime combine beautifully to complement the okra and transform it into an absolutely celestial dish.

Wash and towel-dry the okra. For the success of this dish it is imperative that the okra be completely dry. Cut the okra into approximately 3/4-inch-thick slices.

Heat the oil in a medium pan and add the okra and onion. Cook uncovered, on high heat, for approximately 4 minutes. Stir occasionally.

Mix in the turmeric powder, mustard seeds, chili flakes, and maldive fish if using. Reduce heat to low and season with salt. Cook for another 3 to 4 minutes and stir frequently. Turn off heat, stir in the lime juice, and adjust salt. This dish is best served with steamed white rice and Dhal Curry (page 119).

Variation
Add 1 medium chopped ripe tomato and 1/2 cup coconut milk to the cooked okra and cook, uncovered, on high heat for 4 to 5 minutes. Stir frequently and adjust salt.

3/4 pound fresh young okra
3 tablespoons vegetable oil
1 medium red onion, finely chopped
1/8 to 1/4 teaspoon turmeric powder
1/4 teaspoon mustard seeds
1/2 to 3/4 tablespoon red chili flakes
1 teaspoon maldive fish flakes (optional)
Salt to taste
Fresh lime juice to taste

Tender Jackfruit Pickle

Polos Achcharu   *Serves 6*

This exotic earthy pickle is the perfect blend of sweet, sour, and heat that is intertwined with the flavors of mustard, garlic, and ginger. *Polos Achcharu* is at its best when paired with red country rice.

Peel off the green skin of the *polos*, cut into pieces, and boil in salted water until tender. Cut off the core and finely grind the *polos*. For more texture, pulse for a few seconds in a food processor to achieve a slightly chunky or shredded result.

In a small saucepan combine the chili powder, mustard, garlic, ginger, and vinegar. Bring to a boil, mix well, and season with salt. Add the *polos* and boil uncovered for 3 to 4 minutes. Stir frequently.

Cool to room temperature and mix in the sugar. Let stand a few minutes for the flavors to intermingle.

Tip
An equal quantity of canned young green jackfruit can be substituted for the boiled jackfruit above.

1 small tender jackfruit
   (approximtely 1 1/4 pounds)
   or 1 (20-ounce) can
   (drained weight of 10
   ounces)
Salt to taste
1 to 1 1/2 teaspoons chili
   powder
2 to 3 teaspoons mustard
   seeds, ground or 1 to 1 1/2
   teaspoons mustard paste
3 to 4 large cloves garlic,
   ground to a paste
1 teaspoon finely ground
   fresh ginger
1 cup vinegar
1 teaspoon sugar

Country Cucumber Curry

This humble cucumber preparation is a cooling contrast for a hot and spicy meal. The use of each ingredient is imperative to the success of this soothing dish.

Peel the cucumbers and cut in half lengthwise. Scoop out and discard the seeds and cut each half lengthwise into two. Next cut the four lengths diagonally into relatively chunky diamond shapes.

Heat the oil in a small saucepan, add the cucumber, onion, fenugreek seeds, curry leaves, mustard seeds, turmeric powder, peppercorns, garlic, cinnamon, curry powder, and green chili. Cook on high for approximately 1 minute and stir constantly. Season with salt and pepper.

Stir in the mustard paste and coconut milk. Bring to a boil and adjust salt. Cover and simmer on moderate heat for 10 to 12 minutes. Stir occasionally. This beautiful dish is best served with steamed red rice.

Tip
This recipe will work equally well with both zucchini and snake gourd. Keep in mind, if using snake gourd, to scrape the white covering off. Then, leave the skin on and cut the gourd into relatively small pieces. Since the seeds of both these vegetables add to the overall recipe, it is best to incorporate the seeds.

1 large cucumber
  (approximately 1 pound)
1 tablespoon vegetable oil
1 medium onion, finely
  chopped
8 fenugreek seeds
3 to 4 curry leaves
$1/8$ to $1/4$ teaspoon mustard
  seeds
$1/8$ to $1/4$ teaspoon turmeric
  powder
5 black peppercorns
1 clove garlic, sliced
2-inch stick cinnamon
1 teaspoon raw Sinhala curry
  powder
1 small green chili
Salt to taste
Freshly milled black pepper
  to taste
$1/2$ to $3/4$ teaspoon mustard
  paste
1 cup coconut milk

Karavila (Bitter-Gourd) with Tomatoes

Serves 4 to 6

In this preparation, the inherent bitterness of the gourd is toned down to an enjoyable level. The tomatoes beautifully round off the bitter corners while contributing a depth of flavor and color to the dish.

Cut the *karavila* into approximately ³/4-inch pieces and soak in water for about 40 minutes. Change the water a few times. Boil the *karavila* in plenty of well-salted water until tender. Drain the water.

Heat the oil in a small saucepan. Add the onion, green chili, maldive fish if using, fenugreek seeds, mustard seeds, chili powder, turmeric powder, curry leaves, and cumin seeds. Fry for 20 to 30 seconds on high heat. Stir constantly to prevent burning.

Add the *karavila* pieces along with the chopped tomatoes and season with salt and pepper. Cook on moderate heat for 1 to 2 minutes and stir frequently. Pour in the coconut milk and cook, uncovered, on moderate heat for 8 to 10 minutes. Stir occasionally and adjust salt.

Tip

Once the bitter gourd has been boiled in the salted water, taste and see if it's palatable. If not, simply cut away some of the dark green skin before proceeding (the skin contains most of the inherent bitterness).

1 medium *karavila* (bitter-gourd); (approximately ¹/2 pound)
2 tablespoons vegetable oil
1 small red onion, finely chopped
1 medium green chili, finely chopped
¹/2 teaspoon maldive fish flakes (optional)
6 fenugreek seeds
¹/8 teaspoon mustard seeds
1 teaspoon chili powder
¹/8 teaspoon turmeric powder
4 to 5 curry leaves
¹/8 teaspoon cumin seeds
1 medium ripe but firm tomatoes, chopped
Salt to taste
Freshly milled black pepper to taste
¹/2 cup coconut milk

Stuffed Capsicum Badum

Serves 4 to 6

Fiery hot and delightfully hearty, this capsicum dish will warm your heart and soul while coconut milk, the exotic cooling agent, discretely achieves its goal to perfection.

Place the capsicums in a saucepan, cover with water, season with salt, and bring to a boil. Cook for 2 to 3 minutes, turn off heat, cover and leave for a few minutes. Cut the capsicums on one side lengthwise and scoop out the seeds and white ribs.

Heat 3 to 4 tablespoons oil in a medium pan. Add half of the onion, maldive fish if using, tomato, chili flakes, chili powder, mustard seeds, and turmeric powder. Season with salt and fry on high heat for 40 to 50 seconds. Stir constantly. Add the potatoes and cook on high heat for another 2 minutes. Adjust salt and stir frequently.

Stuff the parboiled capsicums with this potato mixture. Heat the remaining 4 tablespoons oil in a large flat skillet and arrange the stuffed capsicums in a single layer. Sprinkle in the remaining onion and season with salt. Cook uncovered, on moderately high heat for 2 to 3 minutes. Add the coconut milk, cover, and simmer for 8 to 10 minutes. Adjust salt and chili powder.

8 medium-size capsicums
7 to 8 tablespoons
  vegetable oil
2 medium red onions,
  finely chopped
1 teaspoon maldive fish
  flakes (optional)
1 large firm tomato, skinned
  and finely chopped
1/2 teaspoon red chili flakes
1/2 teaspoon chili powder
1/2 teaspoon mustard seeds
1/4 to 1/2 teaspoon turmeric
  powder
Salt to taste
2 large potatoes, parboiled,
  peeled, and finely diced
1/2 cup coconut milk

Variation
When making the filling, add 3 1/2 ounces of canned tuna to the above ingredients. This simple change will deliciously transform the overall flavor of the recipe.

Ash Plantain Curry

This peasant dish will delight you by its sheer simplicity and uninhibited flavor.

Ash Plantain Curry is at its very best when cooked in this conventional style where the ash plantain is gently cooked in a creamy coconut milk sauce.

Peel the skin of the ash plantains and cut on an angle into approximately 1/2-inch-thick slices.

Heat the oil in a small saucepan. Add the onion, green chili, mustard seeds, curry powder, curry leaves, cinnamon, fenugreek seeds, and turmeric powder. Fry for 20 to 30 seconds on high heat and stir continuously to prevent burning.

Add the sliced ash plantains and 2 cups water. Bring to a boil and season to taste with salt and pepper. Cover, and cook on high heat for 12 to 15 minutes. Stir occasionally. At this point the plantains should be cooked through.

Stir in the coconut milk and mustard paste. Adjust salt, and cook, uncovered, on moderate heat for approximately 10 minutes. Ash Plantain Curry is heavenly served with steamed red or white rice and Coconut Sambol (page 58).

Variation
Deep-fry the ash plantain slices until golden brown and then use in the above recipe. Eliminate the cooking in water step by adding the fried plantain to the sautéed onion mix and cooking directly in the coconut milk.

1 pound ash plantains (cooking bananas)
1 tablespoon vegetable oil
1 medium red onion, finely chopped
1 medium green chili, sliced
1/8 to 1/4 teaspoon mustard seeds
1/2 teaspoon raw Sinhala curry powder
3 to 4 curry leaves
2-inch stick cinnamon
8 fenugreek seeds
Pinch of turmeric powder
Salt to taste
Freshly milled black pepper to taste
1 teaspoon mustard paste
1 cup coconut milk

Moong Dhal Curry

Pan-roasting the green gram accentuates its inherent flavors while the delicate yet distinct flavors of fennel, coconut milk, and curry leaves enhance the overall goodness of this simple recipe.

Pan-roast the moong dhal on moderately low heat until golden brown. This should take approximately 10 minutes. Stir frequently to prevent burning.

In a small saucepan combine the dhal, 2 to 2¼ cups water, ¼ of the onion, a few fennel seeds, and turmeric powder. Bring to a boil, season with salt, cover and cook on moderate heat for approximately 15 minutes until the dhal is tender. Stir occasionally and keep an eye on the pot as the preparation has a tendency to overflow.

Heat the oil in a small pan and fry the remaining onion, curry leaves, and green chilies for 20 to 25 seconds. Season with salt and stir in the garlic, remaining fennel seeds, and mustard seeds. Stirring constantly fry for a few seconds and adjust salt.

Together with the coconut milk add the above fried mixture to the saucepan with the dhal. Adjust salt and cook uncovered on moderate heat for approximately 8 minutes. (If preferred stir in ⅛ teaspoon chili powder.)

1 cup moong dhal
   (green gram)
1 medium onion, finely
   chopped
¼ teaspoon fennel seeds
Pinch to ⅛ teaspoon
   turmeric powder
Salt to taste
1 to 2 tablespoons
   vegetable oil
6 to 8 curry leaves
2 medium green chilies,
   roughly chopped
1 large clove garlic,
   finely sliced
¼ to ½ teaspoon
   mustard seeds
½ cup thick coconut milk
   (see page 31)

Mango Curry

Amba Maluwa

This rustic recipe teams the inherent sourness of unripe mango with the distinct flavors of maldive fish, coconut milk, and onion. Mango Curry is especially delicious served with red country rice.

Peel the green skin of the mango and cut into fairly chunky pieces (leave some flesh on the seed). Carefully cut the tough seed in to halves or quarters. If preferred omit using the seed.

In an approximately 6-inch saucepan, combine the mango, onion, green chilies, maldive fish, turmeric powder, curry powder, coconut milk, and cinnamon.

Mix well and season with salt.

Heat the oil in a small pan, take off the heat and add the chili powder, mustard seeds, and curry leaves. Stirring constantly let the ingredients fry (off the fire) in the hot oil. Transfer this mixture to the saucepan with the other ingredients.

Bring to a boil, adjust salt, and cook on moderate heat for approximately 25 minutes, until he mango is tender and the curry thickened (not a runny gravy). Stir occasionally. Leave for a few minutes for the flavors to unify. This mango preparation is well complemented when served with warm Milk Rice (page 74).

Tips
The sourness of the preparation is determined by the variety of mango used and also by the rawness of the fruit.

1 large unripe mango
1 large onion, finely
  chopped
2 medium green chilies,
  cut lengthwise in half
1 tablespoon maldive fish
  flakes
Pinch to $1/8$ teaspoon
  turmeric powder
$3/4$ to 1 tablespoon roasted
  Sinhala curry powder
$1^1/2$ cups coconut milk
2-inch stick cinnamon
Salt to taste
2 to 3 tablespoons
  vegetable oil
1 to $1^1/4$ teaspoons
  chili powder
$1/2$ teaspoon mustard seeds
6 to 8 curry leaves

Keep in mind too that the above factors also determine the cooking time and cooking liquid required.

Plantain Blossom Badum

Kessel Muwa Badum

This perfect plantain flower bud recipe is uniquely Sri Lankan and extremely delicious. The unusual flavors of this country-style recipe are guaranteed to delight and pamper the palate. When in season you can purchase *kessel muwa* in Asian and Oriental grocery stores.

Remove the outer layer of petals of the *kessel muwa*, finely chop, and wash well. Squeeze out the excess water.

Heat the oil in a small saucepan. Add the *kessel muwa*, turmeric powder, onion, chili powder, maldive fish, curry leaves, green chili, and tomato if using. Season with salt and fry on moderately high heat for 2 to 3 minutes. Stir frequently to evenly distribute the ingredients and to prevent burning.

1 medium *kessel muwa* (plantain flower bud)
3 tablespoons vegetable oil
1/8 to 1/4 teaspoon turmeric powder
1 medium red onion, finely chopped
1 teaspoon chili powder
3/4 to 1 tablespoon maldive fish flakes
5 curry leaves
1 to 2 medium green chilies, slit lengthwise
1 small tomato, finely chopped (optional)
Salt to taste
1 cup coconut milk

Mix in the coconut milk and bring to a boil. Adjust salt, cover, and simmer on moderately low heat for 15 to 20 minutes, until tender and moist (non-watery) in consistency. Stir occasionally. This simple and exotic preparation is wonderful served with steamed red rice.

Variation
Boil the cut *kessel muwa* in water seasoned with salt and turmeric powder and cook until tender. Squeeze out the excess water and in a medium saucepan combine with 1/3 to 1/2 cup oil, turmeric powder, 1 tablespoon maldive fish, onion, curry leaves, green chili, and tomato. Season with salt and fry on moderately high heat for approximately 8 minutes. Stir frequently. Add 1 to 1 1/2 teaspoons chili powder and 1/4 cup coconut milk. Adjust salt and cook for another 1 to 2 minutes and stir constantly.

110   **Exotic Tastes of Sri Lanka**

Tender Jackfruit Curry

Polos Curry   *Serves 6*

This wonderfully exotic and beautiful traditional preparation is a definite comfort food. In this dish, the delicate coconut milk and alluring aromatic ingredients enhance the robust flavors of the jackfruit.

Cut off the thick outer green skin of the *polos*. Cut the *polos* into approximately 2-inch pieces. Place in a medium bowl and add the onion, curry powder, 1½ tablespoons chili powder, maldive fish, gamboge, and cinnamon. Mix all the ingredients well and season with salt.

Heat the oil in a medium saucepan. Add the garlic, ginger, curry leaves, pandan leaf, mustard seeds if using, and remaining ½ tablespoon chili powder. Season with salt and fry for approximately 30 seconds on high heat. Stir constantly. Add the *polos* mixture and fry for another 1 to 2 minutes. Adjust salt and stir frequently.

Add the coconut milk, bring it to a boil, and adjust salt. Cover and simmer on low heat for approximately 30 minutes until the *polos* pieces and tender. Stir occasionally. This gorgeous country-style dish is great served with steamed rice, *pappadam*, White Fish Curry (page 167), and Kale Mallum (page 71).

1 small *polos* (tender jackfruit)
1 medium red onion, finely chopped
1 tablespoon roasted Sinhala curry powder
2 tablespoons chili powder
1 to 1½ tablespoons maldive fish flakes
3 cloves gamboge, ground
2-inch stick cinnamon
Salt to taste
1½ tablespoons vegetable oil
3 large cloves garlic, finely sliced
1-inch piece ginger, sliced
5 curry leaves
2-inch piece pandan leaf
¼ teaspoon mustard seeds (optional)
2 to 2¼ cups coconut milk

Pumpkin Kalu Pol Curry

Serves 4

Kalu pol or "blackened coconut" is the essence of this traditional Sri Lankan pumpkin preparation. In this recipe the pumpkin is gently cooked in a magnificent blend of ingredients.

Scoop out and discard the pumpkin seeds and fibers. With its skin on, carefully cut the pumpkin into approximately 2-inch pieces. It is best for each piece to have a side with the skin attached. The skin helps prevent the pumpkin flesh from disintegrating during cooking.

Heat the oil in a medium saucepan. Add the onion, green chilies, turmeric powder, cinnamon, curry leaves, and chili powder. Fry for 20 to 30 seconds and stir constantly. Add the pumpkin pieces together with 1 cup water. Bring to a boil and season with salt. Cover and cook on high heat for 6 to 8 minutes until the pumpkin is cooked through.

While the pumpkin is cooking make the *kalu pol* for the curry by combining the coconut, dry red chilies, garlic, ginger, rice, mustard seeds, fennel seeds, and cumin seeds in a small pan. Stirring constantly, pan-roast until dark brown. With a little water, grind the roasted ingredients to a smooth paste.

To the cooked pumpkin, add the *kalu pol* mixture, curry powder, mustard paste if using, coconut milk, and sugar if using. Bring to a boil, adjust salt, cover, and cook on moderate heat for 8 to 10 minutes. Stir occasionally.

1 pound pumpkin
1 to 2 tablespoons vegetable oil
1 small red onion, finely chopped
1 to 2 medium green chilies, sliced lengthwise in half
1/8 teaspoon turmeric powder
2-inch stick cinnamon
3 to 4 curry leaves
1/2 teaspoon chili powder
Salt to taste
1 tablespoon grated coconut
3 whole dry red chilies
2 cloves garlic, sliced
1-inch piece ginger, sliced
3/4 teaspoon raw rice
1 teaspoon mustard seeds
1/2 teaspoon fennel seeds
1/2 teaspoon cumin seeds
1 to 2 teaspoons roasted Sinhala curry powder
1/2 teaspoon mustard paste (optional)
1 cup thick coconut milk (see page 31)
Pinch of sugar (optional)

Lotus Root Badum

Nelum Ala Badum   *Serves 4 to 6*

This is a dish of absolute beauty and intrigue, where the inherent texture and flavor are truly a unique experience. Lotus Root Badum is especially delicious served with steamed white or red rice.

Boil the lotus roots in salted water. Take off the skin from all sides and cut into fairly thin slices. (The slices will resemble beautiful lace-like flowers.) Place in medium small saucepan and mix in the maldive fish, turmeric powder, half the onion, green chilies, 2 teaspoons chili powder, curry powder, and coconut milk. Bring to a boil, season with salt, and simmer on moderately low heat for approximately 15 minutes. Stir occasionally.

Heat the oil in a medium saucepan. Add the garlic, remaining onion, mustard seeds, and curry leaves. Fry on high heat until the onions are golden-brown and stir constantly. Add the remaining 1 teaspoon chili powder and season with salt. Stir in the cooked curry and cook for 30 to 40 seconds. Adjust salt and stir frequently.

Tip
Canned, sliced lotus root can be successfully substituted for the boiled lotus roots in the above recipe.

1 pound lotus root
Salt to taste
2 to 3 teaspoons maldive fish
   flakes
Pinch to $1/8$ teaspoon
   turmeric powder
1 medium red onion,
   finely sliced
2 medium green chilies,
   chopped
3 teaspoons chili powder
1 tablespoon raw Sinhala
   curry powder
1 cup coconut milk
2 tablespoons vegetable oil
2 cloves garlic, finely sliced
$1/2$ teaspoon mustard seeds
5 curry leaves

Wild Eggplant Curry

Thalana Batu Curry

Thalana batu is a wild variety of eggplant that grows abundantly in tropical climates. This extremely wholesome and deliciously mild vegetable preparation will melt in your mouth as you savor each heavenly bite.

Put the *thalana batu* into a plastic bag. With a heavy object like a rolling pin, bash the bag so as to crush the *thalana batu* open. Wash the crushed *thalana batu* well until all the seeds come out (the seeds often cause itchiness and it is best not to incorporate them in the recipe).

In a medium saucepan combine the *thalana batu*, onion, maldive fish, curry leaves, green chilies, turmeric powder, and coconut milk. Bring to a boil and season with salt. Cover and simmer on low heat until cooked. Stir occasionally.

Heat the oil in a small pan and fry the mustard seeds for a few seconds. Add this mix to the *thalana batu* curry and cook for another 40 to 50 seconds. Adjust salt. This dish is best served over steamed red or white rice.

1 pound *thalana batu* (approximately 1-inch round green-white eggplant variety)
1 small red onion, finely chopped
2 teaspoons maldive fish flakes
5 curry leaves
2 medium green chilies, sliced
1/8 teaspoon turmeric powder
2 to 2 1/2 cups coconut milk
Salt to taste
1 teaspoon vegetable oil
1/4 teaspoon mustard seeds

Traditional Cassava Curry

Serves 4

To many Sri Lankans this heartwarming preparation is a definite comfort food. This wholesome country-style dish is best teamed with steamed rice, Coconut Sambol (page 58), and *Karavala Theldala* (page 175).

Peel the tough skin of the cassava and cut into approximately 1½-inch cubes. Boil the pieces, uncovered, in salted water. Once the cassava is tender (15 to 20 minutes, strain and discard the water.

In a medium saucepan combine the cassava pieces, coconut milk, chopped onion, turmeric powder, green chilies, and curry powder. Bring to a boil, season with salt, and cook on moderate heat for approximately 12 to 15 minutes (until the gravy thickens noticeably). Stir occasionally.

While the curry is simmering, break or cut the dry red chilies into approximately ¾-inch pieces. Heat the oil in a small pan. Add the sliced onion, dry chili pieces, curry leaves, and mustard seeds. Season with salt and fry on high heat for 20 to 30 seconds. Stir constantly. Turn off heat and add the chili powder. Adjust salt. Stir this fried mixture along with the oil into the cooked cassava curry. Cook for another 40 to 50 seconds.

1 pound cassava root
2 cups thick coconut milk
  (see page 31)
1 small red onion,
  finely chopped
⅛ teaspoon turmeric powder
2 small green chilies, sliced
  lengthwise in half
1 teaspoon raw Sinhala curry
  powder
Salt to taste
3 large whole dry red chilies
2 to 3 tablespoons
  vegetable oil
1 small red onion, finely
  sliced
5 curry leaves
½ teaspoon mustard seeds
½ to ¾ teaspoon chili
  powder

Savory Fried Potatoes

Ala Theldala   *Serves 4 to 6*

This spicy fried potato preparation is a guaranteed success. Requiring hardly any cooking time, this delectable recipe is prepared with basic pantry ingredients.

Boil the potatoes in salted water until tender. Peel, let cool, and cut into approximately 1-inch cubes.

Heat the oil in a large skillet. Add the onion, whole chilies if using, curry leaves, mustard seeds, maldive fish if using, turmeric powder, cumin seeds, chili flakes, and coriander powder if using. Fry on high heat for 30 to 40 seconds and stir constantly to prevent burning. Season with salt.

Add the potatoes and cook for another 4 to 5 minutes. Stir frequently with care and adjust salt. When ready, the potatoes should be a beautiful golden brown color.

Variation
The addition of 2 boiled and diced medium carrots, to the above recipe, will introduce a new dimension of flavor and element of color to the recipe.

4 medium potatoes
4 to 5 tablespoons
    vegetable oil
1 large onion, finely sliced
3 to 4 whole dry red chilies
    (optional)
5 curry leaves
$1/2$ teaspoon mustard seeds
$1/2$ teaspoon maldive fish
    flakes (optional)
$1/4$ to $1/2$ teaspoon turmeric
    powder
$1/4$ teaspoon cumin seeds
1 to 2 teaspoons red chili
    flakes
$1/4$ teaspoon coriander
    powder (optional)
Salt to taste

White Potato Curry

Serves 4 to 6

White Potato Curry is wonderfully spiced down and has been a favorite of children for generations. The potatoes are gently cooked in a heavenly coconut sauce and will absolutely melt in your mouth.

Either peel and cut the potatoes into 6 or 8 pieces and boil in salted water, or boil the potatoes in salted water first and then peel and cut them.

Heat the oil in a small saucepan. Add the onion, curry leaves, fenugreek seeds, turmeric powder, tomato if using, peppercorns, mustard seeds, green chili, maldive fish if using, and garlic. Fry for 20 to 30 seconds on high heat and stir constantly.

Mix in the mustard paste and coconut milk and bring to a boil. Season with salt. Add the boiled potato pieces, cover, and cook on moderate heat for approximately 15 minutes. Stir occasionally and adjust salt. (When ready, the gravy should be beautifully creamy and slightly thick.) This potato curry is delicious served in combination with rustic bread and Coconut Sambol (page 58).

Tip
To enable the thickening of the gravy, mash a piece of the cooked potato and stir into the gravy.

2 large potatoes
1 tablespoon vegetable oil
1 medium onion, finely
  chopped
3 curry leaves
6 to 8 fenugreek seeds
$1/4$ teaspoon turmeric powder
1 small ripe tomato,
  chopped (optional)
6 black peppercorns
$1/8$ to $1/4$ teaspoon mustard
  seeds
1 medium green chili, sliced
$1/4$ teaspoon maldive fish
  flakes (optional)
2 cloves garlic, sliced
$1/4$ to $1/2$ teaspoon mustard
  paste
$2 1/2$ to 3 cups thick coconut
  milk (see page 31)
Salt to taste

Northern Eggplant Curry

Vellai Kathirikkai

Serves 2 to 3

This wholesome eggplant recipe originated in the northern region of Sri Lanka. Enjoyed by many, this is an extremely delicious and surprisingly effortless dish to prepare.

Cut the eggplant into approximately 1/2-inch cubes.

Heat the oil in a small saucepan and add the eggplant, onion, green chili, mustard seeds, fenugreek seeds, curry leaves, fennel seeds, and garlic. Season to taste with salt and pepper. Cook on high heat for approximately 2 minutes. Stir constantly to prevent burning.

Pour in the coconut milk together with 2/3 cup water and bring to a boil. Cook, uncovered, on moderately high heat for 18 to 20 minutes. Adjust salt. Stir occasionally towards the end of the cooking time. The final outcome of this dish may not be aesthetic but guarantees tremendous flavor.

1 medium eggplant
  (approximately 3/4 pound)
2 tablespoons vegetable oil
1 small red onion, finely
  chopped
2 medium green chili,
  chopped
1/8 teaspoon mustard seeds
6 fenugreek seeds
3 curry leaves
1/8 teaspoon fennel seeds
2 cloves garlic, finely
  chopped
Salt to taste
Freshly milled black pepper
  to taste
1 cup coconut milk

Traditional Dhal Curry

Parippu Curry   *Serves 4 to 6*

Practically a "must-have" at every meal, there is never a bad time to serve this conventional lentil preparation. It is equally delicious served with either rice or warm rustic bread and the possibilities of this dhal recipe are endless.

Wash the dhal thoroughly with warm water. In a small saucepan, combine the dhal with 2 cups of water and bring to a boil. Add the garlic and turmeric powder and cook on moderately low heat for 6 to 7 minutes. (Keep an eye on the saucepan as the cooking dhal tends to overflow. It helps to leave a spoon in the pot during cooking.)

Season with salt and cook for another 3 to 4 minutes. Add the coconut milk and adjust salt. Stirring frequently, cook for another 6 to 8 minutes.

Heat the oil in a small pan and fry the onions until golden. Add the curry leaves, mustard seeds, cumin seeds, peppercorns, chili powder, and dry chili pieces. Fry for approximately 15 seconds and season with salt. Stir constantly to prevent burning. Pour this fried mixture into the saucepan containing the cooked dhal. Stir and simmer for 40 to 50 seconds. Let rest in the saucepan for a few minutes as this allows the ingredients and their inherent flavors to come together.

1 cup misoor dhal (red lentils)
1 large clove garlic, sliced
$1/8$ to $1/4$ teaspoon turmeric powder
Salt to taste
1 cup coconut milk
3 tablespoons vegetable oil
1 medium onion, finely sliced
5 curry leaves
$1/4$ teaspoon mustard seeds
$1/8$ teaspoon cumin seeds
5 black peppercorns
$1/2$ to 1 teaspoon red chili powder
3 to 4 whole dry red chilies (broken into approximately $3/4$-inch pieces)

Variations

For a thicker and richer version of the dhal curry above, simply reduce the coconut milk to $1/2$ cup and cook as shown. Once cooked, turn off heat and leave for approximately 10 minutes and stir occasionally.

For a nutritious difference, add $1\,1/2$ cups tightly packed spinach leaves to the above recipe together with the coconut milk. Omit adding the fried mixture for this version, but add a chopped medium green chili and onion to the dhal during cooking and season with freshly milled black pepper.

Sinhala Pickle

Sinhala Achcharu   *Serves 6 to 8*

An all-time favorite, this traditional pickle will add a zing to any meal. The wonderfully select blend of ingredients contributes diversity of flavor, texture, and color to the recipe, while the simple vinaigrette ties the elements together.

Julienne the carrots and beans. Cut the papaya into bite-size pieces. Cut the chilies lengthwise 3/4 of the way up into 2 or 3 (depending on the thickness of the chilies).

Separately parboil the onions, papaya, carrots, and beans in 1 1/2 cups vinegar that has been seasoned with salt. Drain the vinegar and place the ingredients in a medium bowl. Mix in the remaining 3/4 cup vinegar, mustard, sugar, and chili powder and season with salt. Mix thoroughly and allow the *achcharu* 1 to 2 days to really come together. Toss occasionally.

Variation

For the Malay pickle, mix in 5 deseeded, roughly chopped dates and an extra 1/2 teaspoon chili powder to the above *Sinhala Achcharu*.

2 large carrots, peeled
6 tender green French beans
1/4 small green papaya,
  peeled and deseeded
10 medium green chilies
20 red pearl onions, peeled
2 1/4 cups vinegar
Salt to taste
1 1/2 tablespoons mustard
  seeds, freshly ground
1 teaspoon sugar
1/4 teaspoon chili powder

Green Bean Curry

In this gorgeous dish, the gentle spices pay homage to the beautiful green beans while both children and adults will surely adore its delicate flavors.

Cut the beans into 1½ to 2-inch pieces.

Heat the oil in a small saucepan. Add the onion, fenugreek seeds, mustard seeds, curry leaves, turmeric power, maldive fish if using, cumin seeds, garlic, peppercorns, and chili if using. Fry for approximately 20 seconds and stir constantly.

Add the beans and mustard paste together with 3 cups water. Season with salt and pepper. Loosely cover and cook on moderately high heat for approximately 15 minutes. Stir in the coconut milk, bring to a boil, and adjust salt. Cook uncovered, on moderate heat for another 3 to 4 minutes. Stir frequently.

This green bean preparation is delicious served with steamed white or red rice.

1 pound green beans
2 tablespoon vegetable oil
1 medium onion, finely
   chopped
6 to 8 fenugreek seeds
⅛ teaspoon mustard seeds
3 to 4 curry leaves
⅛ teaspoon turmeric powder
¼ to ½ teaspoon maldive
   fish flakes (optional)
⅛ teaspoon cumin seeds
1 to 2 cloves garlic, sliced
5 black peppercorns
½ teaspoon chili powder or
   1 medium green chili
   sliced (optional)
½ teaspoon mustard paste
Salt to taste
Black pepper to taste
1 cup thick coconut milk
   (see page 31)

Mushroom Badum

Hathu Badum

Serves 4

This exotic dish emphasizes the earthy flavors and inherent texture of the mushrooms. The unique blend of spices mercilessly envelops the mushrooms and to a vegetarian this recipe will make for an ideal meat substitute.

Cut the large-sized mushrooms lengthwise into 4, the mediums into 2, and use the small ones whole. In a medium saucepan combine the oil, onion, mustard seeds, maldive fish if using, curry leaves, curry powder, and turmeric powder. Fry for 40 to 50 seconds on high heat. Stir constantly to prevent burning.

Add the mushrooms and chili powder. Season with salt and cook on high for 3 to 4 minutes. Stir frequently. Cover and cook on moderate heat for approximately 2 minutes.

Mix in the coconut milk, adjust salt, cover, and cook on moderate heat for 7 to 8 minutes. Make certain that the mushrooms are cooked through. This traditional mushroom preparation is at its best when served with Yellow Rice (page 76).

$3/4$ pound button mushrooms
$2^1/2$ to 3 tablespoons vegetable oil
1 medium red onion, finely chopped
$1/8$ to $1/4$ teaspoon mustard seeds
$1/8$ teaspoon maldive fish flakes (optional)
4 to 5 curry leaves
2 teaspoons roasted Sinhala curry powder
$1/8$ teaspoon turmeric powder
$1/2$ to 1 teaspoon chili powder
Salt to taste
$1/2$ to $3/4$ cup coconut milk

Drumstick Curry

This popular Asian vegetable, when prepared according to this traditional recipe, is delightfully delicious and is a fun favorite of both the young and old. This country-style rustic dish is at its best when teamed with steamed red rice.

With the blade of a knife gently scrape along the length of the drumsticks to remove the tough fibers. Cut the sticks into approximately 3-inch pieces.

Heat the oil in a small saucepan. Add the onion, fenugreek seeds, curry leaves, mustard seeds, peppercorns, garlic, and turmeric powder. Fry for 20 seconds and add the drumstick pieces and mustard paste. Season with salt and, stirring constantly, cook on moderately high heat for 30 to 40 seconds.

Stir in the coconut milk, bring to a boil, and adjust salt. Cover and simmer on moderately low heat for approximately 15 minutes until the drumsticks are cooked.

6 young long drumsticks
1 tablespoon vegetable oil
1 small onion, finely
   chopped
6 to 8 fenugreek seeds
3 to 5 curry leaves
1/4 teaspoon mustard seeds
3 black peppercorns
2 large cloves garlic, sliced
1/4 teaspoon turmeric powder
1/2 teaspoon mustard paste
Salt to taste
2 1/2 cups thick coconut milk
   (see page 31)

POULTRY, EGGS, AND MEATS

The recipes in this chapter are adventurous and span a diverse array of meats, with favorites being chicken, beef, pork, lamb, and mutton. The masterful use of natural tenderizers, exotic herbs and spices, and flavorful thickening agents make these traditional recipes works of culinary perfection. Depending on the preferred outcome in texture and flavor, the preparation of the meats often call for varying cooking methods such as stir-frying, slow cooking or oven baking. Safeguarding the distinct and uninhibited flavors of the meat itself is key to the success of each recipe.

Spicy Chicken Curry

The chicken is marinated and cooked in a wonderful mélange of aromatic spices and heat-inducing ingredients to create this tremendously flavorful entrée.

Make 1 or 2 slash cuts on each piece of chicken (optional step). This allows the marinade to penetrate and flavor the meat. Make the marinade by combining the garlic, ginger, pepper, chili powder, turmeric powder, and curry powder in a medium bowl. Mix in 3 to 4 tablespoons of water and season with salt. Add the chicken parts and make sure all the chicken parts are coated with the marinade. Adjust salt, cover with cling-film and marinate for a minimum of 6 hours in the refrigerator.

Heat the oil in a large saucepan. Add the onion, curry leaves, mustard seeds, cinnamon, cardamoms, cloves, and fenugreek seeds if using. Fry on high heat for 20 to 30 seconds and stir constantly to prevent burning. Add the marinated chicken pieces to form one layer. Cook on moderately high heat for approximately 1 minute per side and brown the pieces on both sides.

Pour in 2 to 3 cups water and add the gamboge if using. Bring to a boil and adjust salt. Cover and cook on moderate heat for approximately 20 minutes. Mix in the coconut milk, cover, and simmer on moderate heat for 15 to 20 minutes. Stir occasionally. Add water if necessary. When ready the meat should be tender, even falling off the bones.

Variation
For a faster result skip the marinating step. The garlic, ginger, pepper, chili powder, turmeric powder, and curry powder can be directly added to the fried onion mixture and cooked for a few seconds. Add the chicken and stir to coat in the spices. Add the water and cook as above.

8 skinless chicken parts (preferably pieces with bone)
1 to 2 teaspoons finely ground garlic
1 tablespoon finely chopped fresh ginger
1 teaspoon freshly milled black pepper
1 tablespoon chili powder
1/4 to 1/2 teaspoon turmeric powder
1 1/2 tablespoons roasted Sinhala curry powder
Salt to taste
4 tablespoons vegetable oil
1 medium onion, finely chopped
6 curry leaves
1/4 teaspoon mustard seeds
2-inch stick cinnamon
5 cardamom pods
5 whole cloves
8 fenugreek seeds (optional)
1 to 2 cloves gamboge (optional)
1 cup coconut milk

Chicken with Capsicums and Tomatoes

Serves 4 to 6

In this piquant chicken preparation, the hot capsicums combine beautifully with the tantalizing tomatoes to contribute tremendous flavor and interest to the chicken.

Make 1 or 2 slash cuts per piece of chicken (optional step). In a medium bowl combine the chili powder, turmeric powder, garlic, ginger, and 2 teaspoons soy sauce together with 3 tablespoons water. Mix well and season with salt. Add the chicken and mix to ensure each piece is coated in the marinade. Adjust salt, cover, and refrigerate for 6 to 8 hours.

Heat 3 tablespoons oil in a medium pan. Add the chicken pieces and cook on moderately high heat for 2 to 3 minutes. Sprinkle in the mustard seeds, cumin seeds, onion, tomatoes, chili flakes, and peppercorns. Fry for 2 to 3 minutes on high heat and stir frequently.

Add the remaining 3 teaspoons soy sauce, coconut milk, and 1/3 cup water. Cook on high for 1 to 2 minutes and adjust salt. Cover and simmer on moderately low heat for 20 minutes. Cut the capsicums on the diagonal into approximately 1 1/2-inch-thick slices. Mix in the capsicums, cover, and simmer for another 15 to 20 minutes. Stir occasionally.

In a small pan heat the remaining 1 tablespoon of oil and fry the dry chili pieces for about 35 seconds. Season with salt and stir constantly. Prior to serving, mix in the fried chili and cashew nuts if using. This chicken recipe is especially delicious served with either Fragrant Fried Rice (page 82) or Yellow Rice (page 76).

6 chicken parts, skinless
1 tablespoon chili powder
1/4 teaspoon turmeric powder
1 teaspoon finely ground garlic
1 tablespoon finely chopped fresh ginger
5 teaspoons soy sauce light
Salt to taste
4 tablespoons vegetable oil
1/2 teaspoon mustard seeds
1/4 teaspoon cumin seeds
1 large red onion, cut into 1-inch cubes
2 medium firm ripe tomatoes, chopped
1 to 2 teaspoons red chili flakes
5 black peppercorns
3/4 cup coconut milk
2 large capsicums
6 to 8 dry whole red chilies, cut into 1-inch pieces
1/3 cup cashew nuts, fried until golden (optional)

Sri Lankan-Style Chicken Stew

Serves 4 to 6

Crowned "the queen of stews," this rustic chicken recipe is an absolute treat. The vegetables combine beautifully with the chicken to yield a dish with incredible simplicity and flavor.

Make 1 or 2 slash cuts per piece of chicken (optional step). Heat the oil in a medium saucepan and add the mustard seeds, turmeric powder, coriander powder, garlic, peppercorns, cloves, cardamoms, cinnamon, curry leaves, and pepper. Season with salt, fry for 15 to 20 seconds and stir constantly. Add the chicken pieces and fry for 30 to 40 seconds.

Take off heat, turn the pieces over, and add the potato and carrot. Return to the heat and pour in 1³/4 to 2 cups water. Mix in the mustard and marmite. Bring to a boil adjust salt and pepper. Cover and simmer on moderate heat for 20 minutes.

Turn pieces over, add the onions and coconut milk. Cover and cook on moderate heat for another 10 minutes. Stir in the cornstarch and cook, uncovered, for 1 to 2 minutes. Increase heat and cook for 2 to 3 minutes to thicken the gravy. Stir frequently and adjust salt, pepper, and mustard.

6 chicken parts, skinless
1 tablespoon vegetable oil
¹/4 teaspoon mustard seeds
¹/8 to ¹/4 teaspoon turmeric powder
¹/4 teaspoon coriander powder
1 large clove garlic, sliced
6 black peppercorns
4 whole cloves
4 cardamom pods
2-inch stick cinnamon
3 curry leaves
¹/2 to 1 teaspoon coarse black pepper
Salt to taste
1 large potato, peeled and cut into 6
1 large carrot, peeled and cut into 1¹/2-inch pieces
1¹/2 to 2 teaspoons mustard paste
¹/2 to ³/4 teaspoon marmite or vegemite
8 baby red onions
³/4 cup thick coconut milk (see page 31)
¹/2 to ³/4 teaspoon cornstarch

Spicy Baked Chicken

Amazingly easy to prepare, this delicious baked chicken recipe is ideal for a busy lifestyle. When the chicken is cooking, the beautiful aromas filtering the air will tickle your senses.

Make 1 or 2 slash cuts on each piece of chicken. Place the chicken in a medium dish and rub in the lemon juice and season with salt. Mix in the curry powder, chili powder, chili flakes, garlic, ginger, and pepper together with 3 to 4 tablespoons water. Adjust salt and ensure the chicken is thoroughly coated with the ingredients. Cover and marinate for 6 to 8 hours in the refrigerator.

Preheat the oven to 375°F. Adjust salt. Line a baking tray with aluminum foil and place the marinated chicken pieces together with the lemon wedges. Pour about 1 teaspoon of oil over each piece of chicken and bake for 40 to 50 minutes.

Cut the onion lengthwise in half and cut each half lengthwise into 3 wedges. Separate into individual layers. Cut the bell pepper into slices (do not include any seeds or white flesh).

Heat the remaining 1 teaspoon oil in a medium skillet. Add the onion, green pepper, cumin seeds, and turmeric powder. Cook on high heat and stir frequently. Season to taste with salt. Cook for 2 to 3 minutes, until slightly caramelized. When 10 minutes of cooking time remain, spread this mixture evenly over the baking chicken. Once cooked, remove from oven, cover with aluminum foil, and let stand for 8 to 10 minutes before serving.

8 chicken parts, skinless
Juice of $1/2$ lemon
Salt to taste
$1\frac{1}{2}$ to 2 tablespoons Jaffna curry powder
1 teaspoon chili powder
1 to 2 teaspoons red chili flakes
1 teaspoon finely ground garlic
$1/2$ to 1 tablespoon finely chopped fresh ginger
Freshly milled black pepper to taste
6 to 8 small lemon wedges
3 tablespoons vegetable oil
1 to 2 medium onions
1 large green bell pepper
$1/8$ to $1/4$ teaspoon cumin seeds
Pinch of turmeric powder

Tip

When time permits marinating the chicken is recommended, but you can also simply skip the marinating time and directly proceed to baking the spice rubbed chicken (and follow as above).

Chicken with Cilantro and Tomato

Serves 4 to 6

This chicken preparation is traditionally served with *Thosai* (page 85). In this dish, the chicken flavor is enhanced by the beautiful flavors of tomato, cilantro, and yogurt.

Cut each chicken thigh across the bone, into 3 pieces. Place the chicken pieces in a medium bowl. Add the curry powder and flour and season with salt and pepper. Mix to ensure all the pieces are well coated.

Heat the oil in a medium saucepan. Add the onion, cilantro, mustard seeds, fenugreek seeds, fennel seeds, cloves, cardamoms, garlic, and ginger. Fry for 1½ to 2 minutes and stir frequently.

Add the chicken pieces and fry on high heat for 1 to 2 minutes, to beautifully brown each piece. Stir frequently to prevent burning. Mix in the tomato and, stirring constantly, cook for another 30 to 40 seconds.

Add 2 cups water and bring to a boil. Add the yogurt, adjust salt, cover, and simmer on low heat for 30 minutes. Add the green chilies and cook, uncovered, on low heat for another 10 to 15 minutes. Stir occasionally and adjust salt.

8 large chicken thighs, skinless
1½ to 2 tablespoons Jaffna curry powder
2 to 3 tablespoons all-purpose flour
Salt to taste
Freshly milled black pepper to taste
3 to 3½ tablespoons vegetable oil
1 medium onion, finely chopped
⅔ cup finely sliced fresh cilantro
½ to ¾ teaspoon mustard seeds
6 fenugreek seeds
Pinch of fennel seeds
3 whole cloves
3 cardamom pods
2 large cloves garlic, finely chopped
½ to 1 tablespoon finely chopped fresh ginger
1 large ripe firm tomato, chopped
2 to 3 tablespoons plain yogurt
3 small green chilies, chopped

130   Exotic Tastes of Sri Lanka

Chicken Livers with Onion and Chili

Chicken liver probably never tasted better than in this stir-fry version. This recipe transforms the livers into a delectable entrée that is absolutely magnificent.

Heat the oil in medium pan. Add the chicken livers and fry on high heat for approximately 1 minute. Stir frequently.

Cook on moderate heat for another 2 to 3 minutes. Add the onion and season with salt. Cover and cook on moderate heat for 3 to 4 minutes. Add the curry leaves, chili flakes, chili powder, mustard seeds, and turmeric powder. Adjust salt and season with pepper and cook on moderately high heat for 6 to 8 minutes. Stir frequently and ensure the livers are cooked through. This simple chicken liver preparation is most enjoyable when served with steamed white rice and Dhal Curry (page 119).

Variation
The addition of coconut milk effortlessly transforms this recipe into a delicious *badum*. Add 1/3 cup of coconut milk to the above liver recipe and, stirring occasionally, simmer for 2 to 3 minutes.

2 to 3 tablespoons vegetable oil
3/4 pound chicken livers, cut into fairly large pieces
1 medium onion, finely chopped
Salt to taste
3 curry leaves
2 teaspoons red chili flakes
1/2 teaspoon chili powder
1/4 teaspoon mustard seeds
Pinch to 1/8 teaspoon turmeric powder
Black pepper to taste

Batter-Fried Chicken

Adults and children alike will savor this beautiful chicken preparation. Batter-Fried Chicken is especially well complemented by hot bread, butter, and an ensemble of steamed vegetables.

Place the chicken legs in a medium saucepan and cover with water. Season the water with turmeric powder to taste, salt, and coarse black pepper. Boil for 10 to 12 minutes and drain the water.

In a medium bowl combine the milk, egg, flour, turmeric powder, coarse black pepper, and chili powder if using. Whisk for a few seconds to mix all the ingredients and form a thick batter. Season with salt and pepper. Add the chicken legs and mix to ensure they are well coated in batter.

Heat the oil in a medium frying pan. To avoid burning the delicious crispy covering, fry the chicken on moderately high heat and, make sure the chicken is cooked through. Drain the excess oil on plenty of absorbent paper and serve immediately.

Variation
For a tremendously flavorful difference add $1/4$ to $1/3$ cup finely chopped fresh cilantro to the batter.

8 chicken legs
$1/8$ teaspoon turmeric powder
   or more to taste
Salt to taste
Freshly milled coarse black
   pepper to taste
1 cup cold 2% milk
1 medium or large egg
1 cup all-purpose flour
$1^1/2$ teaspoons coarse black
   pepper
$1/8$ teaspoon chili powder
   (optional)
Oil for deep-frying

Fried Egg Curry

Serves 4 to 6

Eggs prepared this way will disappear like hot cakes. Extremely flavorful and appetizing, this egg curry is amazingly effortless to prepare.

With a sharp pin, prick the boiled eggs all around. This will prevent the eggs from bursting during frying. In a medium pan, heat 2 tablespoons of oil and add the turmeric powder. Season with salt. Add the whole eggs and fry on moderately high heat for 4 to 5 minutes. Stir constantly. When ready, the eggs will have a gorgeous golden brown color and crispy texture. This process adds an interesting dimension to the recipe.

Heat the remaining 2 tablespoons oil in a small saucepan. Add the onion, mustard seeds, fenugreek seeds, chili powder, curry leaves, and peppercorns. Cook on high heat for approximately 1 minute and stir constantly to prevent burning. Add the tomato and green chili and cook for another 15 to 20 seconds. Season with salt.

Add the coconut milk together with $1/4$ to $1/3$ cup water and bring to a boil. Adjust salt and season with pepper and turmeric powder. Cover and simmer on moderately low heat for 6 to 7 minutes. Sir frequently.

Add the fried eggs (either as whole eggs or cut lengthwise into halves) and simmer for 30 to 40 seconds. This dish is ideal served with Stringhoppers (page 89).

6 medium eggs, hard boiled and peeled
4 tablespoons vegetable oil
$1/8$ teaspoon turmeric powder
Salt to taste
1 small red onion, finely chopped
$1/8$ to $1/4$ teaspoon mustard seeds
6 to 8 fenugreek seeds
$1/4$ teaspoon chili powder
3 curry leaves
5 black peppercorns
1 small ripe firm tomato, finely chopped
1 small green chili, sliced lengthwise
2 cups thick coconut milk (see page 31)
Black pepper to taste

Poached Egg Curry

The eggs in this recipe are poached and cooked to perfection in a wonderfully flavorful and aromatic spiced tomato curry. This dish is best served with warm rustic bread.

Heat the oil in a small nonstick saucepan. Add the onion, mustard seeds, turmeric powder, chili powder, and fenugreek seeds. Fry for approximately 20 seconds and stir constantly. Add the tomato with its liquid and season with salt and pepper. Cook on moderately high heat for approximately 2 minutes. Stir frequently.

Add the coconut milk, bring to a boil, and adjust salt. Take off the heat and as quickly as possible (to ensure the eggs cook at the same rate) break the eggs into four corners of the curry. Before proceeding, make sure that there is plenty of curry liquid to poach the eggs in. If not, add a little water and adjust salt.

Return to heat (if using an open flame, it is best to use a heat dissipater), cover, and simmer on low heat for 6 to 8 minutes. The curry is ready when the egg whites are set and the centers are still soft and creamy. Turn off heat and leave for 8 to 10 minutes before serving.

Tip

As an equally delicious and attractive garnish, sprinkle a pinch of roasted Sinhala curry powder and 1 finely chopped medium green chili (seasoned with salt) over the dished curry.

2 to 3 tablespoons vegetable oil
1 small red onion, finely chopped
$1/8$ teaspoon mustard seeds
Pinch to $1/8$ teaspoon turmeric powder
1 teaspoon chili powder
6 to 8 fenugreek seeds
1 (14-ounce) can diced tomatoes
Salt to taste
Freshly milled black pepper to taste
$1 1/4$ cups coconut milk
4 medium eggs

Sri Lankan-Style Savory Omelet

The *kathurumurunga* flowers (seasonally available in Sri Lankan and Oriental grocery stores) and coconut milk introduce an exotic twist to this all-time egg preparation. This omelet is equally delicious served with warm bread or rice.

Wash and clean the flowers and/or buds, remove stems, and cut into approximately ½-inch lengths, wash and squeeze out the excess water. Sprinkle a pinch of salt on the green chilies and set aside. Break the eggs into a medium bowl and whisk until light and frothy. Whisk in the coconut milk.

Heat the oil in a medium nonstick pan. Add the flowers and/or buds, onion, mushrooms, and tomato. Fry on moderate heat for approximately 3 minutes. Stir frequently to prevent burning. Make sure the ingredients are cooked through.

Add the green chilies and season with chili powder, salt, and pepper. Cook on high heat for 20 to 30 seconds. Stir constantly. Evenly spread the stir-fried mixture and pour the beaten egg. Adjust salt, pepper, and chili powder.

Cook on moderately low heat until the egg is cooked and set. Either flip the omelet over or fold the 2 ends in to form a thick roll and cut into portions. Typically the omelet should be slightly moist and not too dry. Best served warm.

10 to 12 *kathurumurunga* flowers or buds
2 to 3 medium green chilies, finely chopped
6 extra large eggs
1 tablespoon thick coconut milk (see page 31)
Salt to taste
3 to 4 tablespoons vegetable oil
1 medium red onion, finely chopped
½ cup roughly chopped oyster mushrooms
1 small tomato, finely chopped
Pinch to ⅛ teaspoon chili powder or Jaffna curry powder
Plenty of freshly milled black pepper to taste

Tip

For a fun difference individual omelets can be made in a small nonstick pan by using portions of the sautéed ingredients and beaten eggs. May require additional oil for frying the omelets.

Dinner Eggs

The eggs in this recipe are given layers of beautiful texture and flavor while maintaining harmony and simplicity. This preparation makes a lovely dinner entrée and when cut in halves or quarters is an ideal starter.

With a sharp pin, prick the boiled eggs all around. This helps prevent the eggs from bursting during frying. Heat the oil in a small pan and add 1/8 teaspoon turmeric powder. Season with salt and add the boiled eggs. Fry for 2 to 3 minutes on moderately high heat and stir constantly to ensure the eggs are fried to a wonderful crispy golden brown on all sides. Drain the excess oil on plenty absorbent paper.

In a food processor combine the onion, green chili, curry leaves, ground beef, chili powder, and uncooked egg. Season with salt and pepper. Pulse for a few seconds to form a smooth paste-like mixture. Divide the meat mixture into 4. Carefully mold (using the fingers) each portion around an egg to entirely cover that egg.

In a small bowl combine the flour with the remaining 1/8 teaspoon turmeric powder and mix in 3/4 to 1 cup cold water. Mix well to form a thick batter and season with salt and pepper. Carefully dip the meat-covered eggs in the batter and cover with bread crumbs.

Heat the oil and deep-fry on moderately high heat until golden brown. Make sure the meat is cooked. Drain the excess oil on plenty of absorbent paper. These eggs can be made in advance and deep-fried prior to serving.

4 medium eggs, hard boiled
  and peeled
2 tablespoons vegetable oil
1/4 teaspoon turmeric powder
Salt to taste
1 small red onion, finely
  chopped
1 medium green chili,
  finely sliced
2 curry leaves, finely sliced
1/2 pound ground beef
1/4 to 1/2 teaspoon chili
  powder
1 small egg
Freshly milled black pepper
  to taste
1 cup all-purpose flour
1 cup coarse bread crumbs
Oil for deep-frying

Spicy Beef and Potato Curry

Serves 4

Chunky and succulent, this recipe incorporates a plethora of aromatic ingredients. The humble potatoes and delicate coconut milk harmoniously complement the fiery heat of this exquisite curry.

In a medium bowl combine the curry powder, black pepper, chili powder, turmeric powder, garlic, ginger, and vinegar. Season with salt and mix in 2 to 3 tablespoons water. Add the meat and rub the marinade into the meat. Adjust salt. Cover with cling-film and marinate for 6 to 8 hours in the refrigerator.

Heat the oil in a medium saucepan. Add the onion, curry leaves, pandan leaf, cinnamon, peppercorns, cardamoms, cloves, fenugreek seeds, and mustard seeds. Fry for 20 to 30 seconds on moderately high heat and stir constantly. Add the meat and potatoes and fry on high for 30 to 40 seconds. Stir frequently and season with salt.

Add the coconut milk and bring to a boil. Adjust salt, cover, and simmer on moderately low heat for 30 minutes. Cook uncovered, on moderately high heat for approximately 3 minutes. Stir occasionally. Turn off heat, cover, and let stand a few minutes before serving.

Tip
To hasten the preparation simply skip the marinating time and add the spice-rubbed meat directly to the fried onion mixture and continue as above.

2 to 3 teaspoons roasted Sinhala curry powder
$1/2$ teaspoon freshly milled black pepper
2 to 3 teaspoons chili powder
$1/8$ teaspoon turmeric powder
2 large cloves garlic, ground to a paste
2 teaspoon finely chopped fresh ginger
1 teaspoon vinegar
Salt to taste
$1 1/2$ pounds slightly marbled cut of beef (chuck, rump round, shank, etc.), cut into 1-inch cubes
2 tablespoons vegetable oil
1 medium onion, finely chopped
4 to 5 curry leaves
2-inch piece pandan leaf
2-inch stick cinnamon
5 black peppercorns
3 cardamom pods
3 whole cloves
6 fenugreek seeds
$1/4$ teaspoon mustard seeds
1 large potato, peeled and cut into 6
$1 3/4$ cups coconut milk

Beef and Green Pepper Badum

Each mouthful of this promising dish is a medley of flavors working in unison to delight the taste buds. The green peppers add a hint of peppery bite while the beef marinated in spices contributes tremendous flavor to the recipe.

Cut the beef against the grain into thin ($1/8$ to $1/4$-inch thick), moderate-size slices (holding the knife at an angle almost parallel to the cutting board will help). In a medium bowl, combine the beef, curry powder, chili powder, coriander powder, turmeric powder, garlic, ginger, and vinegar. Mix in 1 to 2 tablespoons water and season with salt and pepper. Cover and marinate for a minimum of 3 hours in the refrigerator. For best results marinate for 8 to 12 hours.

Cut the bell pepper lengthwise into half, remove the seeds and white fleshy strands, and slice each half lengthwise into strips. Heat the oil in a medium skillet. Add the curry leaves, cumin seeds, mustard seeds, and the beef slices (at room temperature). Fry on high heat (to brown the meat) for approximately 3 minutes and stir frequently.

Add the bell pepper and onion. Stirring constantly cook on high heat for another 4 to 5 minutes. Season with salt. Pour in the coconut milk, adjust salt and pepper, and stirring frequently, cook on high heat for 2 to 3 minutes. Turn heat off and let stand for a few minutes.

1 pound beef (chuck, round, shank, rump, etc.), preferably with some marbling
2 to 3 teaspoons roasted Sinhala curry powder
1 teaspoon chili powder
$1/2$ teaspoon coriander powder
Pinch to $1/8$ teaspoon turmeric powder
$3/4$ to 1 teaspoon finely ground garlic
$3/4$ to 1 tablespoon finely chopped fresh ginger
1 to 2 teaspoons vinegar
Salt to taste
Freshly milled black pepper to taste
1 medium green bell pepper
3 tablespoons vegetable oil
Small sprig of curry leaves
$1/8$ teaspoon cumin seeds
$1/4$ to $1/2$ teaspoon mustard seeds
1 medium red onion, finely sliced
$1/2$ cup coconut milk

Deviled Beef

Serves 4

This is a delicious sauté of beef, capsicums, red onions, and tomato. The main ingredients are perfectly tied together by the intermingling flavors of coconut milk, red chili, and ginger.

Heat 2 to 3 tablespoons oil in a medium saucepan. Add the meat, turmeric powder, and ginger. Fry on high heat and stir constantly for 2 to 3 minutes. Add the chili paste, chili flakes, capsicums, and onion. Cook on high for approximately 2 minutes and stir frequently.

Add the chopped tomato, season with salt and cook for another 2 to 3 minutes. Stir in the coconut milk, bring to a boil, cover and cook on moderate heat for 8 to 10 minutes. Adjust salt.

In a small pan heat the remaining 2 tablespoons oil and fry the garlic, curry leaves if using, and lemongrass if using for approximately 20 seconds. Add the chili powder, season with salt, and cook for approximately 5 seconds. Stir constantly to prevent burning. Stir this mixture into the cooking meat and cook on high heat for 40 to 50 seconds. Stir constantly. This dish is lovely served with Rice Pilau (page 77).

4 to 5 tablespoons vegetable oil
1 pound beef, cut into $1/2$-inch cubes
Pinch of turmeric powder
1 tablespoon finely chopped fresh ginger
1 to 2 teaspoons red chili paste
$1/2$ teaspoon red chili flakes
2 large capsicums, sliced diagonally 2-inches thick
1 large red onion, cut into 1-inch cubes
1 large ripe firm tomato, cubed
Salt to taste
$2/3$ cup coconut milk
2 large cloves garlic, sliced
Small sprig of curry leaves (optional)
4-inch stem lemongrass (optional)
1 teaspoon chili powder

Liver Curry

Try this spicy liver recipe and you will be hooked for life, as this creative preparation is truly a conventional masterpiece.

Slice the liver $1/3$-inch thick. When slicing it helps to hold the knife at an angle almost parallel to the cutting board.

Place the flour on a plate and season with salt and pepper. Dredge the slices of liver in the seasoned flour.

Heat the oil in a medium pan and add the liver. Fry for approximately 2 minutes per side on moderately high heat. Reduce heat to moderately low and add the coarse black pepper, turmeric powder, and mustard seeds and season with salt and pepper. Cook for approximately 1 minute.

Add the vinegar and onion rings together with 1 to $1 1/4$ cups water. Bring to a boil, cover, and simmer on moderate heat for 12 to 15 minutes. Stir occasionally and adjust salt and pepper. Ensure the liver is cooked through.

Sprinkle on the ginger, green chilies, and cilantro if using. Turn off heat and leave for a few minutes before serving. This recipe is perfect served with warm rustic bread accompanied with a dollop of butter.

1 pound beef liver
$1/2$ cup all-purpose flour
Salt to taste
Freshly milled black pepper
  to taste
4 tablespoons vegetable oil
1 teaspoon coarse black
  pepper
$1/2$ teaspoon turmeric powder
$1/2$ teaspoon mustard seeds
$1/2$ to 1 tablespoon vinegar
1 large red onion, sliced into
  $1/2$-inch rings
$1/2$ tablespoon finely
  chopped fresh ginger
1 to 2 medium green chilies,
  finely sliced
Few cilantro leaves, chopped
  (optional)

Authentic Mutton Curry

This delicious spice-infused mutton preparation has been a source of pride to generations of Sri Lankan cooks. The recipe incorporates unripe papaya, which is one of nature's most exotic tenderizers.

Heat the oil in a medium saucepan and fry the onions for 40 to 50 seconds on high heat. Add the curry powder, chili powder, pepper, turmeric powder, mustard seeds, cumin seeds, fenugreek seeds, cinnamon, cardamoms, cloves, curry leaves, pandan leaf if using, garlic, and ginger. Season with salt and, stirring constantly, fry for approximately 30 seconds.

Add the meat and papaya if using, and cook on high heat for approximately 3 minutes. Stir constantly and adjust salt. Stir in the coconut milk, bring to a boil, readjust salt, cover, and simmer on low heat for about 45 minutes.

Cook uncovered, on moderately low heat for about 15 minutes. Stir frequently. If the curry is running dry, add a little water or coconut milk. Turn off heat, cover, and let stand for a few minutes before serving. This beautiful mutton curry is fabulous served with most traditional staples such as *Pittu* (page 88), Hoppers (page 91), and Stringhoppers (page 89).

Variation

Lamb makes a perfect substitute for the mutton in this recipe. Bear in mind that the cooking time will be slightly less for lamb.

- 2 tablespoons vegetable oil
- 1 medium onion, finely sliced
- 2 tablespoon roasted Sinhala curry powder
- 2 to 3 teaspoons chili powder
- 1 teaspoon freshly milled black pepper
- 1/4 teaspoon turmeric powder
- 1/2 teaspoon mustard seeds
- 1/4 teaspoon cumin seeds
- 6 to 8 fenugreek seeds
- 3-inch stick cinnamon
- 5 cardamom pods
- 5 whole cloves
- Small sprig of curry leaves
- 2-inch piece pandan leaf (optional)
- 6 large cloves garlic, finely chopped
- 1/2 tablespoon finely chopped fresh ginger
- Salt to taste
- 2 1/2 pounds mutton (leg meat is preferred), cut into 1 to 1 1/2-inch pieces (include pieces with bone)
- Few small slices unripe papaya (optional)
- 1 1/2 cups coconut milk

White Mutton Curry

This beautiful Tamil recipe is an absolutely unique culinary experience. The inherent flavors of the ingredients are kept clean and distinctive while the mutton is cooked to perfection.

In a medium saucepan combine the mutton, onion, green chilies, garlic, ginger, curry leaves, turmeric powder, fenugreek seeds, cinnamon, peppercorns, mustard seeds, lime juice, and coconut milk. Mix well to evenly distribute all the ingredients, bring to a boil and season with salt. Cover and cook on low heat for 45 to 50 minutes until tender.

While the meat is cooking, pan-roast separately the fennel seeds and rice flour until brown. Grind the fennel seeds to a powder and mix with the rice flour.

Add the roasted ingredients and thick coconut milk to the meat. Bring to a boil, adjust salt and cook, uncovered, on moderately low heat for 10 to 15 minutes (until the gravy thickens). Stir occasionally. This curry is best served with Stringhoppers (page 89). Garnish with deep-fried finely sliced onion.

Variation
This recipe works well with lamb and chicken. Keep in mind that cooking times will vary depending on the meat. It is best to cook until the meat is tender.

1 1/2 pounds mutton (leg meat is preferred), cut into 1-inch cubes (include pieces with bone)
1 small red onion, finely chopped
3 large green chilies, sliced in half lengthwise (joined at the stem)
4 large cloves garlic, sliced
1 to 2 teaspoons finely chopped fresh ginger
6 curry leaves
1/2 teaspoon turmeric powder
8 fenugreek seeds
2-inch stick cinnamon
6 to 8 black peppercorns
1/4 teaspoon mustard seeds
Juice of 1/2 lime
1 1/2 to 1 3/4 cups coconut milk
Salt to taste
3/4 to 1 teaspoon fennel seeds
3/4 teaspoon rice flour
1/2 cup thick coconut milk (see page 31)

Lamb with Tomatoes

Serves 6

The marriage of lamb and tomatoes never tasted better than when prepared in this simple and delicious recipe. The flavors and fragrance of spices, coconut milk, ginger, and garlic enhance this tremendous dish.

Heat the oil in a medium saucepan and add the onion and fry for 20 seconds on high heat. Add the curry leaves, cinnamon, cloves, cardamoms, cumin seeds, garlic, ginger, coriander powder, turmeric powder, chili powder, and chili flakes. Season with salt and pepper and fry for approximately 10 seconds. Stir constantly.

Add the lamb pieces, tomatoes, and green chilies. Cook on high heat for 6 to 8 minutes and stir frequently. Season with salt. Stir in 1 1/2 cups water and the coconut milk. Bring to a boil, adjust salt, cover, and simmer on moderate heat for 30 to 40 minutes until tender. Stir occasionally.

Turn heat off and mix in the mint leaves if using. Cover and let stand for a few minutes before serving. This lamb preparation is best served over a gorgeous bed of Yellow Rice (page 76).

3 tablespoons vegetable oil
1 medium onion, finely chopped
6 curry leaves
2-inch stick cinnamon
5 whole cloves
5 cardamom pods
1/4 to 1/2 teaspoon cumin seeds
6 large cloves garlic, finely chopped
1/2 tablespoon finely chopped fresh ginger
1 teaspoon coriander powder
1/8 teaspoon turmeric powder
2 teaspoons chili powder
1 teaspoon red chili flakes
Salt to taste
Freshly milled black pepper to taste
2 1/4 to 2 1/2 pounds lamb (leg meat is preferred), cut into 1 to 1 1/2-inch cubes (include pieces with bone)
3 medium ripe firm tomatoes, chopped
2 to 3 medium green chilies, sliced in half lengthwise
1 cup coconut milk
3 to 5 mint leaves (optional)

Minced Meat with Cauliflower and Onion

Ground meat is combined with and complemented by the cauliflower florets and onion slivers. The exotic spices and delicate coconut milk further heighten this recipe.

Cut the onion lengthwise in half. Cut each half lengthwise into 3 wedges and separate the onion layers. Heat the oil in a medium saucepan. Add the onion, cauliflower, turmeric powder, mustard seeds, cumin seeds, whole chilies, and curry leaves. Season with salt and cook on moderately high heat for approximately 1½ minutes. Stir constantly.

Reduce heat and add the ground meat, garlic, ginger, curry powder, chili powder, and coriander powder. Cook on low heat for approximately 2 minutes and stir constantly. Adjust salt, cover and cook on moderately low heat for 12 to 15 minutes. Stir occasionally. This delicious meat preparation can be served with either white rice or warm rustic bread.

1 medium onion
2 tablespoons vegetable oil
1 to 1½ cups small
　cauliflower florets
⅛ teaspoon turmeric powder
½ teaspoon mustard seeds
¼ teaspoon cumin seeds
3 whole dry red chilies
3 curry leaves
Salt to taste
½ pound ground beef
2 large cloves garlic, finely
　chopped
1 teaspoon finely chopped
　fresh ginger
¾ to 1 tablespoon Jaffna
　curry powder
1 to 2 teaspoons chili powder
1 teaspoon coriander powder

Traditional Pork Curry

Serves 4

This delicious authentic Sri Lankan preparation is savored by many. It is especially delicious served with Yellow Rice (page 76).

Pan-roast the fennel and cumin seeds and grind to a powder. In a medium nonstick saucepan combine the roasted ingredients, pork, onion, 2 tablespoons oil, curry leaves, ginger, cinnamon, vinegar, turmeric powder, curry powder, and chili powder together with 2 to 2^1/$_3$ cups water. Mix and season with salt and pepper.

Cover and cook on moderately low heat for 25 to 30 minutes. Add the coconut milk, bring to a boil, and adjust salt. Cover and cook on moderately low heat for 5 to 6 minutes.

Transfer the gravy to a bowl, add the remaining 2 tablespoons oil and let the meat fry on high heat for approximately 2 minutes. Stir constantly. Pour back the gravy and cook for 40 to 50 seconds.

Variation
For a sweet difference, add ^{1}/$_2$ teaspoon brown sugar to the meat during the frying process.

For a simpler preparation, heat the oil and fry the cumin seeds, fennel seeds, onion, curry leaves, ginger, cinnamon, turmeric powder, curry powder, and chili powder for about 20 seconds. Add the meat and cook (to brown) on high heat for 1 to 2 minutes. Stir constantly and season with salt and pepper. Add the water, vinegar, and coconut milk. Bring to a boil, adjust salt, cover and simmer on moderate heat for 30 to 40 minutes (until tender).

^{1}/$_2$ teaspoon cumin seeds
^{1}/$_4$ teaspoon fennel seeds
1^1/$_2$ pounds pork, cut into
   1-inch cubes (include a few
   pieces with bones)
1 medium onion, finely
   chopped
4 tablespoons vegetable oil
3 curry leaves
1 teaspoon finely chopped
   fresh ginger
2-inch stick cinnamon
1 to 2 teaspoons vinegar
^{1}/$_8$ teaspoon turmeric powder
2 tablespoons roasted
   Sinhala curry powder
2 teaspoons chili powder
Salt to taste
Freshly milled black pepper
   to taste
1 cup coconut milk

Pork in Red Curry

Serves 4

This attractive and fiery hot recipe is definitely for the brave and adventurous palate. The beautiful flavors of coconut milk, gamboge, herbs, and spices contribute to its unique taste.

In a small saucepan combine the meat pieces, onion, 3 teaspoons chili powder, turmeric powder, garlic, ginger, cinnamon, fenugreek seeds, gamboge if using, and lemongrass together with 2 cups water. Mix and season with salt. Cover and cook on moderately low heat for approximately 30 minutes.

Add the coconut milk and lime juice. Bring to a boil, adjust salt, cover, and simmer for 8 to 10 minutes.

Heat the oil in a small pan and fry the pandan leaf and curry leaves for 30 seconds on high heat. Take off heat and let the oil cool for 10 seconds (to avoid burning the chili powder), mix in the remaining 1 teaspoon chili powder and season with salt. Pour this mixture into the meat curry. Stirring frequently cook for 2 to 3 minutes on moderately high heat.

1 1/2 pounds pork, cut into
  1-inch cubes
1 small red onion, finely
  chopped
4 teaspoons chili powder
1/8 teaspoon turmeric powder
2 cloves garlic, finely
  chopped
1 teaspoon finely chopped
  fresh ginger
3-inch stick cinnamon
6 fenugreek seeds
1 to 2 cloves gamboge
  (optional)
3-inch stem lemongrass
Salt to taste
1 cup thick coconut milk
  (see page 31)
Juice of 1/2 small lime
2 to 3 tablespoons vegetable
  oil
2-inch piece pandan leaf
5 to 6 curry leaves

Pork Kalu Pol Curry

Serves 4 to 6

This authentic Sri Lankan dish incorporates *kalu pol*, a roasted infusion of coconut, chili, mustard, garlic, and ginger in its preparation. The meat is cooked to perfection in spiced infused coconut milk gravy.

To make the *kalu pol*, in a small saucepan combine the coconut, garlic, ginger, rice, mustard seeds, fennel seeds, cumin seeds, red chilies, and salt. Pan-roast on moderately low heat until dark brown, almost black color. Stir constantly. With a little water grind the roasted ingredients to a paste and adjust salt.

In a moderately small saucepan combine the pork, *kalu pol*, vinegar, curry leaves, lemongrass, pandan, turmeric powder, curry powder, chili powder, vegetable oil, and 2³⁄₄ cups water.

Mix well, bring to a boil, and season with salt. Cover and simmer on moderately low heat for about 40 minutes. Stir occasionally and adjust salt. When ready the meat should be tender and the curry thickened.

2 tablespoons freshly grated coconut
4 to 5 cloves garlic, sliced
2-inch piece ginger, finely sliced
1 1/2 teaspoons raw rice
2 teaspoons mustard seeds
1/2 teaspoon fennel seeds
1 teaspoon cumin seeds
8 whole dry red chilies
Salt to taste
1 3/4 pounds pork, cut into 1-inch pieces (include a few pieces with bone and some fat)
2 teaspoons vinegar
6 to 8 curry leaves
3-inch stem lemongrass
2-inch piece pandan leaf
Pinch to 1/8 teaspoon turmeric powder
1 tablespoon roasted Sinhala curry powder
1 teaspoon chili powder
1 tablespoon vegetable oil

SEAFOOD

Sri Lanka stands in all its majesty as an island in the Indian Ocean and is truly a seafood lover's paradise. Over the years the islanders have skillfully mastered the culinary art of seafood preparation. These are exquisite recipes where the delicate flavors of the sea are complemented by the flavors of the earth. Often a comfort food, traditional recipes such as Fish Ambul-Thiyal, Stuffed Squid Badum, Prawn Curry, and Crab Curry are never upstaged by trendier recipes like Spicy Baked Fish and Baked Crab. The beauty of these tremendously flavorful recipes lies in the choice complementary ingredients, the freshness of the seafood, and the tender loving care their preparation demands.

Piquant Prawn Curry

Serves 4

The ocean is harvested of one of its treasures in order to adorn our tables with this precious authentic prawn curry.

Remove the prawn heads and leave the shells on (the shells protect the prawns during cooking and reduce shrinkage).

Heat the oil in a small or medium saucepan. Add the prawns, onion, tomato, mustard paste, fenugreek seeds, curry leaves, lemongrass if using, green chilies, garlic, ginger, mustard seeds, chili powder, paprika powder if using, and turmeric powder. Season with salt and pepper. Stirring constantly, cook on moderately high heat for 3 to 4 minutes.

Add the coconut milk together with 1 cup water and bring to a boil. Season with lime juice and adjust salt. Cover loosely and simmer on moderate heat for 12 to 15 minutes. Stir occasionally.

Tip
For convenience, the prawns can be cooked with their shells off (best keep the tail shell on, for the shells contribute both flavor and color to the recipe).

20 to 25 medium tiger prawns
3 to 4 tablespoons vegetable oil
1 medium red onion, finely chopped
1 small ripe firm tomato, chopped (optional)
1 teaspoon mustard paste
6 to 8 fenugreek seeds
5 curry leaves
3-inch piece lemongrass (optional)
2 small green chilies, sliced
1 teaspoon finely ground garlic
$1/2$ tablespoon finely chopped fresh ginger
$1/4$ to $1/2$ teaspoon mustard seeds
2 to 3 teaspoons chili powder
1 teaspoon paprika powder (optional)
$1/8$ teaspoon turmeric powder
Salt to taste
Freshly milled black pepper to taste
2 cups thick coconut milk (see page 31)
Fresh lime juice to taste

Prawns with Onion and Chili

This enticing recipe beautifully combines the flavors of the prawn, onion, and chili, while the lime juice binds the recipe together.

Remove the prawn heads and leave the shells on. The shells protect the prawn flesh during cooking and reduce shrinkage. Further, the shells contribute tremendous flavor and enhance the appearance of the finished dish.

Heat the oil in a large skillet. Add the onion, green chilies, mustard seeds, chili flakes, and turmeric powder. Fry on high heat for approximately 40 seconds. Stir constantly.

Add the prawns, chili powder, and garlic. Stirring frequently, cook on high heat for 3 to 4 minutes and season with salt and lime juice. Cook on moderately low heat for approximately 3 minutes. Add the tomato, adjust salt, and cook on low heat for 5 to 8 minutes. Stir occasionally. When cooked, the prawns will acquire an attractive orange hue, curl, and firm.

18 to 20 medium tiger prawns
3 tablespoons vegetable oil
1 large red onion, finely sliced
2 to 3 medium green chilies, sliced lengthwise in half
$1/2$ teaspoon mustard seeds
2 teaspoons red chili flakes
Pinch to $1/8$ teaspoon turmeric powder
$1/2$ to 1 teaspoon chili powder
4 to 6 large cloves garlic, finely chopped
Salt to taste
Fresh lime juice to taste
1 small or medium ripe firm tomato, chopped

Prawns with Eggplant

Serves 4

This conventional recipe is a melting pot of beautiful flavors and intriguing textures. In this preparation, the marriage of prawns and eggplant is a fantastic example of the successful combination of the flavors of the sea and earth.

Cut the eggplant into approximately 2½ by ½-inch pieces. Deep-fry the eggplant pieces until golden brown and drain the excess oil on plenty of absorbent paper.

Remove the prawn heads and shells leaving only the tail shells. Heat the oil in a medium pan. Add the prawns, onion, chili flakes, chili powder, mustard seeds, turmeric powder, curry leaves, garlic, and ginger. Season with salt and pepper and cook on moderately high heat for 3 to 4 minutes. Stir constantly.

Mix in the eggplant, mustard paste, and green chilies. Cook on high for 1 to 2 minutes. Stir frequently. Add the coconut milk, season with lime juice, and adjust salt. Cook for another 40 to 50 seconds on high heat.

1 medium eggplant
16 medium tiger prawns
Oil for deep-frying
2 tablespoons vegetable oil
1 medium red onion, finely chopped
1 to 1½ teaspoons red chili flakes
½ teaspoon chili powder
¼ teaspoon mustard seeds
⅛ to ¼ teaspoon turmeric powder
3 curry leaves
4 large cloves garlic, ground to a paste
½ tablespoon finely chopped fresh ginger
Salt to taste
Freshly milled black pepper to taste
¾ teaspoon mustard paste
3 medium green chilies, sliced lengthwise in half but attached at the stem
¼ cup coconut milk
Fresh lime juice to taste

Prawn Sambol

This exotic Sri Lankan sambol is a medley of delicious flavors and is surprisingly simple to prepare. The recipe is at its best when served with the delicate Stringhoppers (page 89).

Wash the dried shrimp thoroughly to ensure there are no grains of sand and pan-roast for a few minutes until dry and firm and pound lightly. In a medium bowl combine the coconut, ginger, garlic, coriander powder, and chili powder. Mix and season with salt and pepper.

Heat the oil in a medium skillet. Add the shrimp and onion and fry on moderate heat for approximately 5 minutes. Stir frequently.

Bring 1³/₄ to 2 cups water to boil in a medium saucepan and add the coconut mixture, turmeric powder, mustard seeds, curry leaves, peppercorns, lime juice, and green chilies. Adjust salt and pepper, cover, and cook on moderate heat for 2 to 3 minutes. Stir frequently.

Add the stir-fried shrimp, adjust salt and pepper, cover, and simmer on moderate heat for approximately 5 minutes. The final consistency of this tremendously flavorful dish should be moist but not watery.

1/2 pound small dried baby shrimp
2 cups grated coconut
1 teaspoon finely ground fresh ginger
1 teaspoon finely ground garlic
1 teaspoon coriander powder
1/2 to 1 teaspoon chili powder
Salt to taste
Freshly milled black pepper to taste
2 tablespoons vegetable oil
1 small onion, finely chopped
1/4 to 1/2 teaspoon turmeric powder
1/4 teaspoon mustard seeds
8 to 10 curry leaves
8 to 10 black peppercorns
Juice of 1 medium lime
3 to 4 medium green chilies, sliced lengthwise

Prawn Vadai

Makes 10

Vadai are dumpling-like savory treats made of lentils and are known to be of South Indian origin. Prawn Vadai are uniquely Sri Lankan and an absolutely versatile treat; they can be served as an appetizer, snack, or finger-food.

Sprinkle a pinch of salt over the chopped green chilies and let stand. Drain the water and place 1 1/2 to 1 2/3 cups of the chana dhal in a blender. Blend to form a smooth paste and transfer to a medium bowl. Add the turmeric powder, chili powder, and ground prawns if using. Mix to evenly distribute all the ingredients.

Mix in the green chilies, remaining chana dhal, curry leaves, and onion. Season with salt and divide into 10 equal portions. Form portions into oval shapes and slightly flatten. Securely stud each portion with a small prawn.

Heat the oil in a deep saucepan. Fry on moderate heat until golden brown. Ensure that the *vadai* are cooked through. Drain excess oil on plenty of absorbent paper. *Minchi Sambol* (page 59) makes an ideal accompaniment to these delicious savory prawn treats.

Variation

A simple chana dhal *vadai* can be prepared by substituting 1 to 2 teaspoons of maldive fish flakes for the prawns (both whole and ground) in the above *vadai* mixture.

Salt to taste
3 medium green chilies, finely chopped
2 cups chana dhal, soaked in water for 3 hours
1/8 teaspoon turmeric powder
1 to 2 teaspoons chili powder
4 medium tiger prawns, shelled and finely ground (optional)
6 large curry leaves, finely sliced
1 medium red onion, finely chopped
10 small prawns, with shells
Oil for deep-frying

Exotic Tastes of Sri Lanka

Prawns with Pepper and Long Beans

Serves 4

The prawns are beautifully flavored with crushed black pepper, garlic, ginger, and lime. The long beans contribute an intriguing depth of flavor, texture, and hue. The subtle use of soy sauce hints at ties to the Orient.

Wash and clean the prawns but leave the shells and heads on. (Remove the long feelers and eyeballs.) Using a small sharp knife, carefully cut along the back shells and remove the veins.

Heat the oil in a large pan and add the prawns. Cook on high heat for approximately 3 minutes. Add the peppercorns, long beans, half the onion, garlic, ginger, turmeric powder, and slices of lime. Cook on high heat for 1 to 1½ minutes and stir constantly. Add the soy sauce and season with lime juice and salt.

Reduce heat, sprinkle in the remaining onion, cover, and cook on moderate heat for approximately 3 minutes. Adjust salt and stir occasionally. Ensure the prawns are cooked through. If not, add 2 tablespoons of water, cover, and cook for another few minutes. Leave for a few minutes before serving.

12 large tiger prawns
4 tablespoons vegetable oil
½ to 1 tablespoon crushed black peppercorns
6 to 8 long beans, cut into approximately 2-inch pieces
1 large red onion, finely chopped
3 large cloves garlic, chopped
2 teaspoons finely chopped fresh ginger
⅛ teaspoon turmeric powder
2 to 3 fine slices lime
½ to 1 tablespoon light soy sauce
Fresh lime juice to taste
Salt to taste

Tip
The prawn heads are left on entirely for presentation and if preferred need not be incorporated in the recipe.

Traditional Sri Lankan Crab Curry

To a seafood lover this authentic crab preparation is truly ambrosia. The delicious blend of spices and herbs mingle with the delicate crabmeat to enhance and complement the inherent flavor of the crabs.

Pan-roast the mustard seeds, fennel seeds, and cumin seeds and grind to a powder.

Remove the outer shells of the crabs. Wash and clean the crabs. Break the crab claws and some of the legs from the body. With a hammer or the back of a knife, carefully crack the claws open. Also break the crab bodies into halves but if the crabs are small, leave as is. These procedures allow the flavorful curry to penetrate and flavor the meat.

In a medium deep saucepan combine the crab, onion, tomato, green chilies, garlic, ginger, half the curry leaves, mustard, fennel, cumin, 3 teaspoons chili powder, fenugreek seeds, and turmeric powder. Season with salt and stirring constantly cook on high heat for approximately 2 minutes.

Add the coconut milk, season with salt, and bring to a boil. Reduce heat and cook on moderate heat for 10 minutes. Stir constantly. Cover and simmer on moderate heat for 15 to 20 minutes and add half of the parsley. (Parsley makes an ideal substitute for the traditionally used drumstick leaves, which are unfortunately rarely available in the West.)

Cover and cook for another 15 to 20 minutes on moderate heat. Stir occasionally and adjust salt. Add the rice flour and remaining parsley and cook, uncovered, on high heat for 10 to 12 minutes. The gravy should start to thicken at this point.

Heat the oil in a small pan and add the remaining curry leaves, fry for a few seconds, take off the heat, and mix in the remaining 1 teaspoon chili powder. Stir this mixture into the curry and cook on high heat, stirring frequently for 1 to 2 minutes. Cover and leave for a few minutes before serving.

2 teaspoons mustard seeds
1 teaspoon fennel seeds
1 teaspoon cumin seeds
6 medium blue crabs
1 medium red onion, finely chopped
1 large ripe tomato, chopped
6 small green chilies
5 to 6 large cloves garlic, ground to a paste
1 tablespoon finely ground fresh ginger
A small sprig of curry leaves
4 teaspoons chili powder
10 fenugreek seeds
1/4 teaspoon turmeric powder
Salt to taste
6 cups coconut milk
1 to 1 1/2 handfuls crinkly parsley, chopped
1 to 2 teaspoons white rice flour
2 to 3 tablespoons vegetable oil

Deviled Crabs

Serves 4

This devil of a recipe is wickedly seductive and is for the daring adventurer. The beautiful bouquet of spices complements the delicate crabmeat and will leave you craving for more.

Remove the outer shells and break the crabs at the joints. Cut the body pieces into halves and with a hammer or the back of a heavy knife carefully crack the shells on the other pieces (this step is optional). Cut the capsicums on the diagonal into approximately 2-inch-thick slices.

Heat the oil in a large skillet. Add the crab, onion, garlic, ginger, mustard seeds, chili powder, chili flakes, and turmeric powder. Fry on high heat for 2 minutes and stir constantly.

Mix in the capsicum, tomatoes, soy sauce, and leeks. Season with salt and cook on high heat for approximately 5 minutes and stir frequently. Add the coconut milk, adjust salt, cover, and simmer for 15 minutes. Ensure that the crabs are cooked through; if not, add a little water or coconut milk and cook for another few mintues. Sprinkle on the coriander powder.

6 medium blue crabs
3 large capsicums
4 to 5 tablespoons
   vegetable oil
1 large red onion, chopped
4 large cloves garlic, sliced
1 tablespoon finely chopped
   fresh ginger
$1/2$ to 1 teaspoon mustard
   seeds
2 to 3 teaspoons chili
   powder
1 teaspoon red chili flakes
Pinch of turmeric powder
2 medium firm ripe
   tomatoes, cubed
2 tablespoons light soy sauce
$3/4$ cup julienned leeks
Salt to taste
$1/3$ cup coconut milk
1 teaspoon roasted coriander
   powder

Baked Crab Delight

Serves 4

The western world meets the eastern world to bring you this harmonious and beautiful crab delicacy. With flourish and finesse the ingredients blend to contribute new depths of flavor and texture to this crab recipe.

Separate the outer shells of the crabs and break the crabs at the joints. Clean and boil the crabs and outer shells separately in salted water. Extract both the dark and white meat.

Preheat the oven to 350°F. In a medium saucepan combine the crabmeat, butter, onion, green chilies, garlic, and ginger. Season with salt and plenty of pepper. Cook on moderately high heat for 1 to 2 minutes and stir constantly to prevent burning.

Add the tomato and cook for another 30 to 40 seconds. Stir in the potato, adjust salt and pepper, and cook until the mixture comes together (do not let it dry out). Take off the heat. Mix in 1 tablespoon cheese and the parsley. Fill the crab shells with the mixture and pat on the bread crumbs to cover.

In a small bowl combine the egg, milk, and remaining cheese. Mix well and season with salt and pepper. Spoon this over the bread crumb coverings and bake for approximately 20 minutes until a beautiful golden brown crust forms. Serve warm.

4 large crabs
1 1/2 to 2 tablespoons butter or margarine
1 medium red onion, finely chopped
3 to 4 medium green chilies, finely chopped
2 large cloves garlic, ground to a paste
1/2 to 1 teaspoon finely ground fresh ginger
Salt to taste
Freshly milled black pepper to taste
1 small tomato, finely chopped
1 medium potato, boiled, peeled, and mashed
1 tablespoons finely chopped parsley
1/3 cup grated cheddar cheese
1/2 cup coarse bread crumbs
1 extra large egg, beaten
1/3 to 1/2 cup whole milk

Spicy Fish Curry

The fiery hot gravy introduces a new dimension to the delicate flavors of the sea, while the exotic spices intertwine discretely to balance the overall flavors of this recipe.

Heat the oil in a small saucepan. Add the onion, turmeric powder, curry leaves, mustard seeds, fenugreek seeds, chili powder, garlic, pepper, gamboge, cinnamon, lemongrass, and pandan. Season with salt and cook on high heat for approximately 20 seconds. Stir constantly to prevent burning.

Add the fish and cook on moderately high heat for approximately 1 minute. Stir frequently.

Add the coconut milk, bring to a boil, and adjust salt. Cover and simmer on moderately low heat for 10 to 12 minutes. Ensure the fish is cooked through. Stir occasionally and adjust salt.

Variation
For a spicier flavor substitute 2½ cups coconut milk for the thick coconut milk. This will also result in a less rich gravy.

2 to 3 tablespoons vegetable oil
1 medium red onion, finely chopped
Pinch to ⅛ teaspoon turmeric powder
3 large curry leaves
¼ teaspoon mustard seeds
8 fenugreek seeds
1½ tablespoons chili powder
4 large cloves garlic, sliced
½ teaspoon freshly milled black pepper
2 cloves gamboge, finely ground
2-inch stick cinnamon
3-inch piece lemongrass
2-inch piece pandan leaf
Salt to taste
1 pound fish (king mackerel preferred), cut into thick pieces
3½ cups thick coconut milk (see page 31)

Spicy Baked Fish

Serves 4 to 6

A mélange of conventional spices and refreshing lemon juice is infused with the fish to give a unique edge to this popular baked fish recipe. In this beautiful recipe a deliciously spicy edible crust protects the fish while the delicate flesh is gently cooked to perfection.

Gut and clean the fish and leave on the heads. With a sharp knife, make 3 to 4 (on a slant) deep slashes approximatel; 3-inches apart on each side of the fish. This will enable the flavors to penetrate the fish. Pan-roast the cumin seeds, fennel seeds, and coriander seeds. Grind to a powder and transfer to a small bowl.

Preheat the oven to 375°F. To the toasted ingredients add the pepper, chili flakes, chili powder, ginger, vinegar, soy sauce, and turmeric powder. Mix in 1 to 2 tablespoons water and season with salt. Apply this mixture on the fish and make sure to season the incisions and the stomach cavities. Adjust salt. Place the lemongrass in the stomach cavity.

Pat the bread crumbs to cover the fish on both sides and inside the stomach cavity. Drizzle the melted butter and season with lemon (on both sides). Place the fish in a baking dish. Bake for 15 to 20 minutes until browned, cover with aluminum foil, and bake for another 15 to 20 minutes. Ensure the fish is cooked through. Let stand for a few minutes before serving.

Tip
This recipe will work with most fish types. If using an oily fish such as jack mackerel, it is advisable NOT to use butter in the recipe.

2 medium whole fish (total weight 2 pounds); (Spanish mackerel, trout, jack mackerel, sea bass recommended)
2 teaspoons cumin seeds
2 teaspoons fennel seeds
2 teaspoons coriander seeds
1 to 2 teaspoons freshly milled black pepper
1 teaspoon red chili flakes
1 teaspoon chili powder
$1/2$ to 1 tablespoon finely chopped fresh ginger
1 to 2 tablespoons vinegar
1 tablespoon light soy sauce
$1/4$ teaspoon turmeric powder
Salt to taste
3 to 4-inch piece lemongrass
1 to $1^{1}/2$ cups coarse bread crumbs
3 to 4 tablespoons butter, melted
Fresh lemon juice to taste

Vara

*V*ara is a simple and rustic fish recipe that incorporates green chili, onion, and coconut in its preparation. This Tamil dish is particularly enjoyable when teamed with red country rice.

Place the fish in a saucepan, cover with water, and bring to a boil. Season the water with turmeric powder, salt, pepper, and vinegar if using. Boil the fish until cooked. Drain the water and remove any skin and bones. With the fingers gently shred the fish. We are looking for a flaky consistency.

Heat the oil in a medium nonstick saucepan. Add the onion, green chili, mustard seeds, and curry leaves. Fry on moderately high heat for 40 to 50 seconds until the onion turns a golden brown. Stir frequently and season with salt and pepper.

Add the garlic, ginger, and coconut. Cook for another minute and stir frequently to prevent burning. Adjust salt. Add the fish and curry powder. Cook on moderately low heat for approximately 1½ minutes. Stir constantly. Turn off heat and mix in a good squeeze of lime. Let rest a few minutes before serving.

1 pound king mackerel steak (Spanish mackerel, halibut, swordfish, tuna)
Pinch of turmeric powder
Salt to taste
Freshly milled black pepper to taste
Vinegar to taste (optional)
2 tablespoons vegetable oil
1 medium or large onion, finely chopped
4 medium green chilies, roughly chopped
½ teaspoon mustard seeds
6 curry leaves
2 to 3 large cloves garlic, ground to a paste
1 teaspoon finely ground fresh ginger
3 to 3½ tablespoons finely grated coconut
¾ teaspoon Jaffna curry powder
Fresh lime juice to taste

Twice-Cooked Fish

Serves 4

Here is a unique dish and genuine treat to the taste buds. The fried fish is gently simmered in a heavenly curry that is flavored with exotic spices, herbs, and tamarind. This country-style dish is especially delicious served with steamed red rice.

Rub the fish slices with the turmeric powder, salt, and pepper. Deep-fry the fish slices in hot oil until golden brown. Drain the excess oil on plenty of absorbent paper.

Pan-roast the cumin and fennel seeds and grind to a powder. In a small saucepan, combine the roasted ingredients, onion, garlic, ginger, chili powder, fenugreek seeds, tamarind paste, lemongrass, curry leaves, and coconut milk. Mix well, bring to a boil and season with salt. Cover and simmer on moderate heat for approximately 5 minutes.

Add the fried fish and cilantro if using, cover, and cook for another 3 to 5 minutes. Adjust salt.

Variation
To the curry, add approximately $1/2$ cup deep-fried 1-inch pieces of young okra along with the fried fish.

1 medium (1 pound) jack
  or Spanish mackerel, sliced
  1-inch thick
$1/4$ teaspoon turmeric powder
Salt to taste
Freshly milled black pepper
  to taste
Oil for deep-frying
$1/2$ teaspoon cumin seeds
$1/2$ teaspoon fennel seeds
1 small red onion, finely
  chopped
3 large cloves garlic, finely
  chopped
1 teaspoon finely chopped
  fresh ginger
3 teaspoons chili powder
6 fenugreek seeds
1 teaspoon tamarind paste
3-inch stem lemongrass
3 curry leaves
2 to $2^1/4$ cups thick coconut
  milk (see page 31)
Salt to taste
Few fresh cilantro leaves,
  sliced (optional)

Fish and Mushroom Pie

The medley of flavors in this east-meets-west dish comes together harmoniously. This simple bake with its layers of flavor is a guaranteed treat to all.

Place the fish in a saucepan, cover with water, and bring to a boil. Season with salt, pepper, turmeric powder, and vinegar if using. Boil until cooked. Remove skin and bones and separate into small pieces. Season with salt and pepper. Should yield a minimum of 2 cups fish.

In a moderately small nonstick saucepan combine the oil, mushrooms, tomato, green chilies, onion, and chili powder. Season with salt and pepper and cook on moderately high heat for approximately 5 minutes. Stirring frequently to prevent burning. Turn off heat and let rest.

In a small bowl combine the potato, 1 tablespoon butter, and 2 tablespoons milk. For easier incorporation it is best to do this while the potato is warm. Season with salt and pepper. Take an approximately 9 by 4-inch round or square ovenproof dish (such as Pyrex) and layer the potato at the base. Next layer the fish, fennel leaves if using, mushroom mixture, 1/2 cup cheese, and macaroni respectively. Pour the egg evenly over the assembly.

Preheat the oven to 350°F. In the same saucepan the mushrooms were cooked combine the remaining butter and milk. Add the garlic and flour and bring to a boil. Season with salt and pepper and cook on moderate heat for about 1 minute until slightly thickened. Stir constantly. Take off heat and stir for another few minutes. Pour this sauce over the assembled ingredients evenly. Sprinkle the remaining cheese and the bread crumbs. Carefully tap the dish down on a counter to compact the ingredients. Gently press down with the back of a large spoon.

Position on the center rack and bake for approximately 25 minutes until golden brown. Let rest a few minutes for the flavors to unify. Best served warm. This dish can be considered a meal in itself and also an accompaniment to a special rice menu.

1 to 1^1/$_2$ pound king mackerel steak (Spanish mackerel, halibut, swordfish, cod, trout)

Salt to taste

Plenty of freshly milled black pepper to taste

Pinch of turmeric powder

1 teaspoon vinegar (optional)

1^1/$_2$ tablespoons vegetable oil

2 cups roughly chopped oyster or button mushrooms

1 small tomato, finely chopped

2 to 3 medium green chilies, finely chopped

1 medium onion, finely chopped

^{1}/$_2$ to 1 teaspoon chili powder

1^1/$_2$ large potatoes, boiled, peeled, and mashed

2^1/$_2$ tablespoons butter

1 cup 2% milk

2 tablespoons chopped fennel leaves (optional)

1^1/$_4$ cups grated cheddar cheese

1^1/$_4$ cups cooked macaroni

1 large egg, beaten

1 clove garlic, finely chopped

1^1/$_2$ to 2 teaspoons all purpose-flour

2 tablespoons bread crumbs

Anchovies with Okra and Tamarind

Nethali Theeyel

Serves 4 to 6

This traditional Tamil recipe has come down many generations delighting each with its unique flavors. In this preparation, the inherent flavors of okra and tamarind work together perfectly to complement that of the anchovies.

Cut the anchovy heads off, gut, and clean well. Heat the oil in a medium saucepan and add the curry leaves, green chilies, onion, mustard seeds, turmeric powder, and fenugreek seeds. Fry on high heat for 40 to 50 seconds and stir constantly.

Dissolve the tamarind paste in 1 cup water and add to the fried ingredients. Bring to a boil and add the anchovies in a single layer. Add the okra and cook on moderately high heat for 1 minute.

Add the coconut milk, bring to a boil, and season well with salt and pepper. Cover and cook on moderately high heat for 5 minutes, adjust salt (bearing in mind that the traditional dish is fairly salty) and cook, uncovered, for 12 to 15 minutes.

Variation
For a modern twist to this conventional recipe, substitute 3 small green tomatoes (chopped) for the tamarind solution. The green tomatoes transform the dish and will be savored by all.

12 to 15 moderately large anchovies
1 to 1$^{1}/_{2}$ tablespoons coconut oil or vegetable oil
5 curry leaves
2 medium green chilies, chopped
1 small red onion, finely chopped
$^{1}/_{4}$ teaspoon mustard seeds
$^{1}/_{4}$ to $^{1}/_{2}$ teaspoon turmeric powder
5 fenugreek seeds
$^{3}/_{4}$ to 1 teaspoon tamarind paste
4 ounces tender okra, cut in 1$^{1}/_{2}$-inch pieces
1 cup coconut milk
Salt to taste
Freshly milled black pepper to taste

White Fish Curry

Serves 4

In this recipe, the mild turmeric-flavored coconut gravy delicately caresses the tender flesh of the fish. This fish preparation is a wonderful accompaniment to Stringhoppers (page 89) and is equally successful served with either warm rustic bread or samba rice.

Heat the oil in a small saucepan. Add the onion, turmeric powder, mustard seeds, gamboge if using, green chili, fenugreek seeds, curry leaves, lemongrass, peppercorns, garlic, and ginger. Season with salt and pepper and fry on high heat for 20 to 30 seconds. Stir constantly to prevent burning.

Add the fish and cook on moderately high heat for approximately 1 minute. Stir frequently. Mix in the coconut milk and mustard paste.

Bring to a boil and season with salt and pepper. Cover and simmer on moderately low heat for 10 to 15 minutes. Ensure the fish is cooked through. Sprinkle on the roasted curry powder if using.

Tips

You can substitute 3½ cups coconut milk for the thick coconut milk without compromising flavor.

This recipe also works well with Spanish mackerel and anchovies.

3 tablespoons vegetable oil
1 medium red onion, finely chopped
¼ to ½ teaspoon turmeric powder
½ teaspoon mustard seeds
1 clove gamboge (optional)
1 medium green chili, chopped
8 fenugreek seeds
5 curry leaves
3-inch stem lemongrass
6 black peppercorns
4 large cloves garlic, sliced
1 teaspoon finely chopped fresh ginger
Salt to taste
Freshly milled black pepper to taste
2 pounds fish (king mackerel preferred), cut into thick pieces
3½ to 4 cups thick coconut milk (see page 31)
½ to 1 teaspoon mustard paste
¼ teaspoon roasted Sinhala curry powder (optional)

Fish Ambul-Thiyal

Delightfully diverse, this conventional Sri Lankan recipe has for generations been a source of great pride in the southern regions of the country. Traditionally cooked in a clay pot, this noble yet humble fish preparation is guaranteed to contribute an intriguing depth of flavor to your meal.

In a medium saucepan combine the fish, gamboge, onion (if using), pepper, chili powder, cinnamon, garlic, green chilies, curry leaves, and 2 to 2½ cups water. Mix thoroughly to evenly distribute all the ingredients and season with salt. Arrange the fish pieces in a single layer, to ensure even cooking.

Cook uncovered on moderate heat for 15 to 18 minutes. Occasionally turn the pieces of fish to coat in the thickening gravy. Drizzle on the oil and vinegar. Adjust salt and cook for another 3 to 5 minutes. Fish Ambul-Thiyal is traditionally prepared in a clay pot and is best served with *Kiri Bath* (page 74).

Variation

Fry 1 large sliced onion and 1 to 2 sliced capsicums in 2 tablespoons oil for approximately 1 minute. Season with salt, pepper, pinch of turmeric powder (optional), and chili powder. Add the Fish Ambul-Thiyal and a little water and cook for 1 to 2 minutes on moderately high heat. Stir frequently.

Tips

A variety of fish can be used in this recipe, but the most common is tuna. Also try swordfish, shark, anchovies, and sardines. When cooking small fish like anchovies, gut the fish and cut off the heads, arrange the whole fish in an orderly fashion in the saucepan or clay pot, and cook.

1 pound tuna fish steaks, cut into 1½-inch pieces
5 to 8 cloves gamboge, finely ground
1 small red onion, finely chopped (optional)
1 to 1½ teaspoons freshly milled black pepper
1 teaspoon chili powder
2-inch stick cinnamon
2 to 3 large cloves garlic, sliced
3 medium green chilies, sliced lengthwise, joined at the stem
5 curry leaves
Salt to taste
1 to 2 tablespoons vegetable oil
1 tablespoon vinegar

This recipe can be successfully prepared in an oven. Preheat the oven to 350°F and bake, uncovered, for 25 to 30 minutes.

Fish Intestine and Roe Badum

Maalu-Bada Badum *Serves 4*

The flavors in this classic badum are wonderfully intense. The beautiful red onions together with the sassy spices enhance the overall goodness of this unique preparation.

Wash and clean the fish intestines, stomach and roe. Cut into medium-sized pieces and place in a medium bowl. Add the onion, green chilies, curry powder, chili powder, and turmeric powder. Mix the ingredients well and season with salt and pepper.

Heat the oil in a small saucepan and fry the curry leaves and mustard seeds for 20 seconds. Stir in the above ingredients, adjust salt, cover, and cook on low heat until cooked, 15 to 20 minutes. Stir occasionally. This recipe is best served with steamed white or red rice.

1 pound fish intestines, stomach and roe (preferably king mackerel or tuna)
2 large onions, finely sliced
2 medium green chilies, sliced
1 teaspoon roasted Sinhala curry powder
1 teaspoons chili powder
$1/8$ turmeric powder
Salt to taste
Freshly milled black pepper to taste
3 to 4 tablespoons vegetable oil
3 curry leaves
$1/4$ teaspoon mustard seeds

Fish in a Fried Onion and Tomato Sauce

Serves 4

The delicately fried fish is bathed in a beautiful spicy infusion of fried onion, chili flakes, and tomato sauce. This versatile preparation can be served with a variety of staples such as Fragrant Fried Rice (page 82), Stringhopper Pilau (page 90), and Tamarind Rice (page 78).

Cut and remove any skin, and cut the fish into approximately 1-inch cubes. Cut out and discard any bones. Place the fish in a small bowl and season with salt, pepper, turmeric powder, and 1/2 to 2/3 tablespoon vinegar. Mix well and rub the seasoning into the fish. Set aside for a few minutes and let marinate.

In a small bowl combine the remaining vinegar, tomato sauce, and 1 1/3 cups water. Mix well and season with salt and chili powder. Heat the oil and deep-fry the fish until golden brown. Drain the excess oil on plenty of absorbent paper.

Heat the 2/3 to 3/4 cup oil in a medium non-stick saucepan. Add the onions and fry on high heat for approximately 2 minutes, until golden brown. Season with salt, add the fish, and stirring constantly fry for another 20 to 30 seconds.

- 1 1/4 pounds kingfish steak (Spanish mackerel, swordfish, tuna, halibut, etc.)
- Salt to taste
- Plenty of freshly milled black pepper to taste
- Pinch to 1/8 teaspoon turmeric powder
- 1 1/2 to 1 2/3 tablespoons vinegar
- 6 to 8 tablespoons tomato sauce or ketchup
- 1/2 to 1 teaspoon chili powder
- Oil for deep-frying
- 2/3 to 3/4 cup vegetable oil
- 3 medium onions, finely sliced
- 1 teaspoon to 2 tablespoons red chili flakes

Take off the heat, add the chili flakes, and season with salt. Return to heat, continue stirring, and allow the chilies to fry for a few seconds. Pour in the tomato mixture and cook for another 40 to 50 seconds. Stir constantly and adjust salt and chili powder. Turn off heat and leave for a few minutes for the flavors to amalgamate.

Breaded Fried Fish

Serves 4 to 6

This fried fish preparation is a great way to introduce children to the nutritious flavors of the sea. The bread crumb crust protects the delicate flesh during cooking and contributes an interesting texture and layer of flavor.

Clean and cut the fish into approximately 3/4-inch-thick slices. In a medium bowl combine the flour, turmeric powder, egg, vinegar, and 1 cup water. Mix thoroughly and season this thick batter with salt and pepper.

Dip the fish slices in the batter and then cover the slices of fish with the bread crumbs. Pat the bread crumbs firmly on.

Heat the oil in a frying pan and deep-fry the fish until golden brown. To ensure the fish is cooked through, it is best if the oil is not extremely hot but moderately so. Also, to avoid the fish from going soggy, do NOT over-crowd the pan.

Drain the excess oil on absorbent paper. This fish recipe is best served with the classic combination of rice, Coconut Sambol (page 58), and Dhal Curry (page 119). It is equally good served with warm rustic bread.

1 to 1 1/2 pounds king mackerel, jack mackerel, or Spanish mackerel
1 cup all-purpose flour
1/8 to 1/4 teaspoon turmeric powder
1 large egg
1 to 2 teaspoons vinegar
Salt to taste
Freshly milled black pepper to taste
1 1/2 to 2 cups coarse bread crumbs
Oil for deep-frying

Fish Sauté

Serves 4

Quick and foolproof to prepare, this dish is a thing of beauty. The black pepper, red onion, vinegar, and coconut milk combine perfectly to enhance the sweet flavors of the sea.

Cut the fish into approximately 1-inch-thick slices. Heat the oil in a large nonstick pan and season with turmeric powder and salt. Add the fish slices and cook on moderately high heat until golden brown for 1 to 2 minutes. Turn the pieces over and add the onion rings, green chilies, mustard seeds, and garlic. Season with salt and pepper to taste and cook for another 2 to 3 minutes.

While the fish is cooking, in a small bowl combine the vinegar, mustard paste, 1/2 teaspoon pepper, coriander powder, together with 1/3 to 1/2 cup water. Mix and season with salt. Pour this mixture over the fish and add the tomato. Cook on a moderately high heat for 6 to 8 minutes.

Adjust salt and cook on high heat for approximately 30 to 40 seconds. This fish recipe is excellent served with warm rustic bread.

1 1/2 pounds king mackerel
4 to 5 tablespoons vegetable oil
1/8 to 1/4 teaspoon turmeric powder
Salt to taste
2 medium red onions, sliced into rings
5 medium green chilies, sliced lengthwise
1/2 teaspoon mustard seeds
2 large cloves garlic, sliced
1/2 to 1 teaspoon freshly milled black pepper
1 tablespoon vinegar
2 teaspoons mustard paste
3/4 teaspoon coriander powder
1 medium ripe firm tomato, skinned and chopped

Country-Style Fried Fish

Makes 10

This scrumptious fried sardine recipe is an absolute favorite of mine and I recommend it without a second's hesitation. Gently flavored with delectable spices the fish is cooked to crispy perfection.

Gut and clean the fish, leaving the heads and tails on.

In a medium bowl combine the vinegar, flour, chili powder, turmeric powder, and black pepper. Mix well and season to taste with salt. Add the fish and stir to thoroughly coat the fish with the seasoning mixture. Adjust salt.

Heat the oil in a fairly deep pan. Fry the fish in batches on moderately high heat until lovely and crispy. Ensure the fish is cooked through. Drain the excess oil on plenty of absorbent paper.

This fish preparation makes a delicious finger-food and is absolutely heavenly served with steamed samba rice.

10 medium-size sardines
1 to 1 1/2 tablespoons vinegar
1 teaspoon all-purpose flour
1 teaspoon chili powder
1/8 to 1/4 teaspoon turmeric powder
1/2 to 3/4 teaspoon freshly milled black pepper
Salt to taste
Oil for deep-frying

Traditional Dry-Fish Curry

Karavala Curry   Serves 4 to 6

Probably one of the most popular Sri Lankan comfort foods, this dry-fish curry is both unique and intriguing. This most humble of recipes is traditionally served with steamed red rice.

Wash and clean the dry fish and ensure there are no grains of sand. Cut the thick skin off and cut into approximately 2 by 1-inch pieces. If cooking anchovy *karavala*, remove heads and use as whole.

Heat ½ tablespoon oil in a small saucepan. Add the onions, curry leaves, mustard seeds, fenugreek seeds, turmeric powder, 1 to 1½ teaspoons chili powder, tomato, green chilies, ginger, garlic, and cinnamon. Fry on high heat for 20 to 30 seconds and stir constantly to prevent burning.

Mix in the coconut milk, bring to a boil, and add the *karavala*. Season with salt and keep in mind that the *karavala* is already very well salted (the anchovy *karavala* may need more salt). Cover and simmer on moderately low heat for 5 to 20 minutes and stir occasionally. The cooking time will vary depending on type of fish, piece size, and how well the pieces have been dried. Heat the remaining 1½ tablespoons oil in a small pan, take off the heat, and add the remaining 1 teaspoon chili powder, and add this mixture to the curry. Cook for another 30 seconds.

½ pound *karavala* (dry fish, such as king mackerel, *katta*, or anchovies); include pieces with bone
2 tablespoons vegetable oil
1 small red onion, finely chopped
5 curry leaves
¼ teaspoon mustard seeds
10 fenugreek seeds
⅛ teaspoon turmeric powder
2 to 2½ teaspoons chili powder
1 medium ripe firm tomato, chopped
3 small green chilies, sliced half way up
1 teaspoon finely ground fresh ginger
3 to 4 large cloves garlic, ground to a paste
2-inch stick cinnamon
2½ to 3 cups coconut milk
Salt to taste

Dry-Fish Theldala

Karavala Theldala   *Serves 4 to 6*

Dry fish cooked according to this timeless recipe is amazingly quick to prepare. This intensely flavorful stir-fry is most enjoyed served in the classic combination of steamed rice, Dhal Curry (page 119), and Coconut Sambol (page 58).

Wash and clean the *karavala*, cut the skin off, and cut approximately ³/₄-inch cubes. If using anchovies, remove the heads, leave as whole and clean thoroughly.

Heat the oil in a small skillet. Take off the heat and carefully add the *karavala* pieces. Return to heat and cook on moderately high heat for approximately 10 minutes until golden brown and crisp. Add the onions, curry leaves, and mustard seeds. Cook for another 10 to 12 minutes on moderate heat. Season with salt and bear in mind that the *karavala* is already quite salty.

Add the chili powder and chili flakes. Stir constantly for approximately 30 seconds. Add the tomato if using, adjust salt, and cook for 1 to 2 minutes and stir frequently. This *karavala* preparation is also wonderful served with warm *Kiri Bath* (page 74).

¹/₂ pound *karavala* (dry fish, such as king mackerel, *katta*, or anchovies)
4 tablespoons vegetable oil
2 to 3 medium red onions, finely sliced
5 curry leaves
¹/₂ teaspoon mustard seeds
Salt to taste
¹/₂ teaspoon chili powder
1 to 1¹/₂ teaspoons red chili flakes
1 medium ripe firm tomato, chopped (optional)

Variation

For a crunchy consistency, separately deep-fry the *karavala* pieces and sliced onion prior to using in the above recipe. Combine the fried ingredients in a small pan together with the curry leaves, mustard seeds, chili powder, and chili flakes. Season with salt and fresh lime juice and stirring constantly cook on high heat for approximately 1 minute.

Traditional Squid Curry

Serves 4 to 6

This conventional recipe is the first image that comes to a Sri Lankan mind when thinking about squid. In this dish, the unique texture and flavor of squid is complemented to the height of perfection by the blend of spices the recipe demands.

Cut the squid into approximately 1½-inch-thick rings.

Heat the oil in a medium saucepan. Add the onion, curry leaves, pandan leaf, cinnamon, lemongrass, fenugreek seeds, chili powder, mustard seeds, pepper, green chili if using, curry powder, turmeric powder, gamboge, garlic, and ginger. Season with salt and fry on high heat for approximately 30 seconds. Stir constantly.

Add the squid (saved tentacles too) and fry 1 minute on moderately high heat. Stir frequently and add the coconut milk together with ¾ to 1 cup water. Bring to a boil, adjust salt, loosely cover, and simmer on moderately low heat for 15 to 18 minutes. Stir occasionally.

1 pound squid, cleaned (save some of the tentacles)
2 tablespoons vegetable oil
1 medium red onion, finely chopped
3 to 5 curry leaves
2-inch piece pandan leaf
3-inch stick cinnamon
3-inch stem lemongrass
6 to 8 fenugreek seeds
1½ to 2 tablespoons chili powder
¼ teaspoon mustard seeds
1 teaspoon freshly milled black pepper
1 small green chili, sliced (optional)
2 teaspoons roasted Sinhala curry powder
⅛ teaspoon turmeric powder
3 to 5 cloves gamboge, finely ground
3 large cloves garlic, ground to a paste
1 teaspoon finely chopped fresh ginger
Salt to taste
2 cups thick coconut milk (see page 31)

Stuffed Squid Serenade

Serves 4

An all-time favorite with my family, this squid preparation is intriguing and delicious. This recipe is wonderfully wholesome and heartwarming and is especially good served with steamed samba rice or Yellow Rice (page 76).

Heat 1½ to 2 tablespoons oil in a small skillet. Add the chopped onion, potato, ⅛ teaspoon turmeric powder, mustard seeds, tomato, green chili, and ½ teaspoon chili powder. Season with salt and pepper and cook on moderately high heat for approximately 5 minutes. Stir frequently. Let cool for a few minutes.

Stuff the squid ¾ ways up with the filling and close each open end with a toothpick. Heat the remaining 2 tablespoons oil in a medium nonstick saucepan. Add the curry leaves and curry powder and season with a pinch of turmeric powder and chili powder. Add the sliced onion and stuffed squid and cook on moderately high heat for 5 to 6 minutes. Adjust salt and pepper and stir frequently (rolling the squid around to color evenly).

Mix in any remaining stuffing, cook for a few seconds longer and turn off heat. Remove toothpicks before serving.

Variation
For a further dimension of exquisite flavor and texture, simply substitute ⅓ cup cooked moong dhal (whole, unhusked) for half the quantity of potato.

3½ to 4 tablespoons
  vegetable oil
1 medium red onion,
  ½ finely chopped and
  ½ finely sliced
1 large potato, parboiled,
  peeled, and finely diced
⅛ teaspoon turmeric powder
  or more to taste
⅛ teaspoon mustard seeds
1 small firm ripe tomato,
  finely chopped
1 medium green chili, finely
  chopped
½ teaspoon chili powder
  or more to taste
Salt to taste
Freshly milled black pepper
  to taste
12 medium squid, cleaned
12 toothpicks
5 curry leaves
½ teaspoon roasted Sinhala
  curry powder

DESSERTS

Sri Lanka, a nation with a sweet tooth, takes its desserts and sweetmeats
very seriously indeed. These heavenly delicious puddings are uncomplicated
and simply a breeze to concoct, while the delicious flavor of coconut
is the essence of many. The sweet fragrant flavors of exotic spices such as
cinnamon, cardamom, and clove are used to enhance and embody many
a dessert. As the desserts vary in key ingredients and cooking methodology
so do texture, flavor, and consistency. For instance,
the beautiful fresh Avocado Pudding is smooth as silk and deliciously
creamy while the steamed Wattalappam Pudding is
sweetly spiced and densely rich.

Avocado Pudding

This pudding is seductively creamy, appealingly vibrant, and heavenly delicious. Amazingly simple to prepare, it has delighted many generations.

Cut the avocados into halves and remove the stones. With a spoon, scoop out the delicious green flesh of the fruits and transfer to a medium bowl.

For a chunky consistency, gently mash the avocado with a fork or for a silky smooth consistency, blend the avocado to a puree.

Add the milk and condensed milk. Mix thoroughly and season with lime juice and salt if using. As this tropical desert is best served cold, cool in a refrigerator until chilled, about 3 hours.

3 large ripe firm avocados
1/3 cup whole milk
Sweetened condensed milk
  to taste
Fresh lime juice to taste
Pinch of salt (optional)

Variation
For a welcome twist to this exotic dessert, substitute the sweetened condensed milk with either grated *kithul* jaggery (palm sugar), *kithul* treacle, or sugar.

Wood Apple Cream

Divul Kiri   *Serves 4*

This dessert is a delicious and intriguing treat to the taste buds. The creamy coconut milk and exotic jaggery heighten the unique inherent flavors of this typically dry-zone fruit.

Crack the tough shell of the wood apples in half. Scoop out the insides and transfer to a medium bowl. When wood apples are perfectly ripe the insides will be a very dark brown-black color. Be sure to scrape every little bit of flavorful pulp off the shells.

Mix in 1 to 1½ cups water and the coconut milk. Mix thoroughly to dissolve the wood apple pulp in the solution. Place a sieve over another medium bowl and pass the wood apple-water mixture through the sieve. With the back of a spoon gently apply pressure on the wood apple mass caught by the sieve. Only the seeds and fibers should be left in the sieve.

4 large ripe wood apples
2½ cups thick coconut milk
  (see page 31)
Finely grated *kithul* jaggery
  (palm sugar) or *kithul*
  treacle to taste
Salt to taste

Add the jaggery, mix well, and season with salt. The final consistency should be rich and fairly thick, but drinkable. Refrigerate until chilled, about 3 hours.

Tip
For a quicker result, use canned wood apple cream/pulp mixed with jaggery (or treacle), coconut milk, and water to achieve the final consistency as above.

Sugar (preferably brown) can be used as sweetener instead of the jaggery.

Tropical Fruit Salad

Serves 6

A medley of exotic fruits, this refreshing spiced salad will make a perfect finale to a heavy and rich meal. The select combinations of fruits contribute a variety of complementary textures and flavors while the aromatic spices and refreshing lime bind the elements together.

Cut the papaya lengthwise into halves. Scoop out and discard the seeds and fibrous mass. Make approximately 1-inch cubes by cutting a grid of 1-inch squares on each half of the papaya and carefully scoop out or cut out the sweet papaya. Place the papaya pieces in a large bowl.

Peel and cut the mango into bite size-pieces and transfer to the bowl with the papaya. Cut the bananas into cubes and season with lime juice (to add flavor and reduce discoloration). Now add the bananas to the bowl along with the pineapple cubes.

Add the mango pulp if using, cinnamon, cloves, and cardamoms. Mix well and season with salt. If using, add the vanilla extract, raisins, and mint. Mix and adjust lime juice. Cover and refrigerate until chilled, about 3 hours. (If necessary season with sugar.) This tropical fruit salad is delicious served topped with either vanilla ice cream, custard, or sweetened condensed milk.

1 small ripe papaya
1 large ripe mango
2 to 3 large ripe bananas
Fresh lime juice to taste
1 to 1½ cups cubed fresh or
  canned pineapple
2 tablespoons mango pulp
  (optional)
Pinch of ground cinnamon
Pinch of ground cloves
Pinch of ground cardamom
Salt to taste
1 to 2 drops vanilla extract
  (optional)
1 to 2 tablespoons raisins
  (optional)
1 mint leaf, finely sliced
  (optional)

Sago Pudding

Satisfyingly wholesome, this appetizing traditional dessert is a definite comfort food. The beautiful pearly granules of sago and the luscious coconut milk define this tasty treat.

Place the sago in a medium saucepan. Add the milk and coconut milk. Cook on medium heat for 10 to 12 minutes and stir occasionally. When cooked, the sago will turn from opaque to translucent.

Sweeten with grated jaggery or sugar and simmer for another 5 minutes. As the tapioca begins to thicken, stir frequently to prevent burning. Add vanilla extract, cinnamon, cloves, cardamoms, and salt. Mix well and cook for another 20 to 30 seconds, stirring constantly.

This simple dessert can be served both warm and cold. To serve warm, it is best to take it off the heat before fully thickened and still runny with a porridge-like consistency. To serve cold, transfer the thickened mixture to a serving dish, cool to room temperature, and refrigerate until set and chilled, about 3 hours.

1/2 cup quick-cooking sago beads or tapioca
1 cup 2% milk
1 cup thick coconut milk (see page 31)
1 tablespoon unsalted butter
Grated jaggery (palm sugar) or sugar to taste
1 drop vanilla extract
Pinch of ground cinnamon
Pinch of ground cloves
Pinch of ground cardamom
Pinch of salt

Variation

For a flavorful difference add 3/4 to 1 tablespoon finely chopped fresh ginger preserve and some of its syrup to the cooking sago.

Tip

If using the slow-cooking type of sago, it is advisable to soak it overnight in water before using in this recipe.

Caramel Pudding

This simple crème brûlée has crossed many borders to tease and delight Sri Lankan taste buds. Always prepared with great love, this beautiful spiced caramel pudding has been cherished for generations.

In a blender or medium bowl place the condensed milk, eggs, vanilla extract, and ground spices together with 2 condensed milk cans of water. Blend or mix with an electric mixer for 1 to 2 minutes. Ensure all the ingredients are well blended. It is best if not many bubbles are formed. Place the sugar and 3 tablespoons water in a deep Pyrex dish or bowl and microwave (on high power) for a minute first and then 25 seconds at a time until a dark golden brown caramel sauce is formed. Rotate the bowl to swirl the caramel and coat the base and sides of the bowl with the caramel sauce. Allow the caramel 1 to 2 minutes to solidify.

Carefully pour in the blended mixture into the caramel-coated bowl. Microwave for 3 minutes on high power and then continue to microwave for a minute at a time for 6 minutes, followed by 30 seconds at a time until the pudding is set. After each cooking, examine the pudding for doneness. When ready, the pudding should be set and slightly wobbly. The total microwave cooking time for the pudding will be 10 to 12 minutes.

Let the pudding cool to room temperature, cover, and refrigerate for a minimum of 4 hours. For best results cool for 6 to 8 hours.

1 (14-ounce) can sweetened condensed milk
5 medium eggs, at room temperature
$1/4$ to $1/2$ teaspoon vanilla extract
Pinch of ground cloves
Pinch of ground cardamom
Pinch of ground cinnamon
3 tablespoons sugar

Variations

The conventional Caramel Pudding is either baked or steamed and has a smooth texture. Using the same ingredients (substituting 8 large eggs) as above, make the blended mixture. Preheat the oven to 350°F. Either make the caramel sauce as above in the microwave (use an ovenproof dish) or make it in a small saucepan (using double quantities) on the stove. If cooking on the stove, do not disturb until it turns a pale golden color and then stir constantly until the sauce turns a dark golden brown and transfer to a warmed ovenproof dish and swirl the sauce to coat the bowl. (It is imperative that the bowl is warm for if not, as soon as the sauce hits the bowl it may solidify and you will be unable to swirl it.) Carefully add the blended mixture to the bowl, cover with greased paper (cut to size), and place the bowl in a baking tin (filled with approximately 1 inch of water). Bake for 60 to 90 minutes, until set.

To steam, place either a trivet rack or a folded dish cloth in the base of a large saucepan. Carefully place the bowl with the pudding mixture and fill the saucepan with water (to reach $2/3$ of the way up the bowl). Bring the water to a rapid simmer, cover, and steam until set. Replenish the water as required. Cool to room temperature and refrigerate until chilled. The pudding is served inversed onto a shallow plate.

An alternate mixture for the conventional methods can be made by combining $4^{1}/_{2}$ cups 2% milk, 1 to 2 tablespoons sugar, and 10 to 11 medium eggs. Season to taste with freshly grated nutmeg and vanilla extract. Bake or steam as above.

Pineapple Fluff

Light as air and wonderfully refreshing, this beautiful pudding is full of promises to come. Pineapple Fluff in all its glory is best described as a pineapple lover's paradise.

Place the unopened can of evaporated milk in a pot of boiling water and boil for 10 to 15 minutes. Cool to room temperature and freeze for 1 to 2 hours. In a medium bowl, combine the evaporated milk, condensed milk, cream of tartar, and food color. Whisk until it approximately doubles in volume. In a small bowl combine the gelatin and 3 tablespoons of the pineapple liquid. Leave until required.

Cut the pineapple into very small pieces. In a medium heatproof bowl combine the yolks, sugar, and 1/2 cup of the pineapple liquid. Place over a pot of simmering water and whisk for 6 to 8 minutes until thickened. An electric hand mixer can be used for the whisking. Take off heat and whisk in the gelatin.

Gradually stir in the egg mixture to the whisked evaporated milk. Fold in the cashew nuts and pineapple pieces and make sure they are evenly distributed. Transfer to a serving dish and refrigerate until set and chilled.

1 (12-ounce) can
  evaporated milk
2 to 3 tablespoons
  sweetened condensed milk
1/4 teaspoon cream of tartar
1 to 2 drops yellow
  food color
2 leveled teaspoons gelatin
1 (15-ounce) can pineapple
  rings, reserved liquid
2 large egg yolks, beaten
1 tablespoon sugar
1/3 cup finely chopped
  cashew nuts

Tip
Never use fresh pineapple in this recipe as it has a tendency to keep the gelatin from setting.

Honey-Coconut Crepes

Pani Pol Crepes   *Makes 12*

These traditional Sri Lankan crepes will melt in your mouth while the heavenly *pani pol* filling is guaranteed to leave you craving more. These delectable crepes not only make a fabulous dessert but also an ideal teatime treat.

To make the filling, in a medium saucepan combine the coconut, jaggery, rice flour, cinnamon, nutmeg, salt, and 1/2 cup of water. Cook on low heat for approximately 8 minutes and stir constantly. The jaggery will melt into the coconut and when ready the rich *pani pol* will have a sticky, smooth, and soft (not hard and toffee-like) consistency and be a deep golden brown hue.

In a medium bowl combine the flour, milk, eggs, butter, and a pinch of salt. Mix well to form the crepe batter. Divide the batter into two and color one portion a very pale-green and the other a rose-pink.

Lightly grease a nonstick crepe pan with butter. Pour in a small portion of the batter to make an approximately 7-inch very thin crepe. Each crepe will take (on low heat) 30 to 40 seconds to cook. Adjust heat to ensure the crepes do not burn.

While warm, immediately place approximately 2 teaspoons of the *pani pol* filling along one side of the crepe and starting from that end, roll the crepe to enclose the filling. Do this with both the pink and green crepes. These delicacies can be served either warm or at room temperature.

1 1/2 cups grated coconut
1 1/2 cups grated jaggery
   (palm sugar)
3/4 teaspoon rice flour
1/4 teaspoon ground
   cinnamon
Freshly grated nutmeg,
   to taste
Pinch of salt
1 cup all-purpose flour
1 cup cold whole milk
2 small eggs
2 tablespoons unsalted
   butter, melted
Pinch each red and green
   powdered food color or
   1 drop each of liquid
   food color

Date Cake

20 to 25 servings

Here is an exotic recipe that ties the unique flavor and texture of dates and pan-roasted semolina with an array of aromatic spices. This beautiful rich moist cake is heavenly savored with a cup of freshly brewed tea or coffee.

Pan-roast the semolina on moderately low heat until golden brown. Preheat the oven to 350°F.

Combine the sugar, butter, eggs, vanilla extract, and brandy in a medium bowl. Whisk well until light and fully blended. Stir in the dates and cashew nuts.

In a small bowl combine the flour, semolina, baking powder, cloves, and cinnamon. Mix well to evenly distribute the ingredients. Gradually add this mixture to the date and nut mixture.

Transfer the cake batter to a greased approximately 8 by 8 by 2-inch square nonstick baking pan, position on the center rack, and bake for approximately 30 minutes. When ready, a toothpick inserted in the middle should come out clean and the cake a beautiful golden brown hue. Cool for a few minutes and remove from tin and cool on a rack to room temperature.

Tip
It is best to use semi-soft dates in this recipe.

2 tablespoons semolina
1/3 to 1/2 cup dark brown sugar
4 tablespoons unsalted butter, at room temperature
4 extra large eggs, at room temperature
1/4 teaspoon vanilla extract
1 tablespoon brandy or dark rum
3 1/2 tightly packed cups finely chopped dates
1/2 cup chopped cashew nuts
2/3 cup all-purpose flour, sifted
1/2 to 3/4 teaspoon baking powder
1/4 teaspoon ground cloves
1/8 teaspoon ground cinnamon

Wattalappam Pudding

Serves 6 to 8

This popular pudding is a highly cherished contribution of the Muslim community to the nation's culinary repertoire. The beautiful flavors of jaggery, coconut milk, and exotic spices make this rich dessert an absolute masterpiece.

All ingredients should be at room temperature. Combine the jaggery, eggs, coconut milk, spices, and salt in a blender. Blend on high speed for approximately 1 minute. Strain and transfer the blended mixture to a heatproof (Pyrex or stainless steel) medium bowl and evenly sprinkle the cashew nuts on top.

To steam, place either a trivet rack or a folded dish cloth in the base of a large saucepan. Carefully place the bowl with the pudding mixture in the saucepan and fill the pan with water (to reach about $2/3$ of the way up the bowl). Bring the water to a rapid simmer, cover, and steam for 25 to 35 minutes. Replenish the water as required. When ready the pudding will be firm to the touch and slightly wobbly.

Cool to room temperature, cover, and refrigerate for 2 to 3 hours until chilled. The pudding can be served inversed onto a shallow platter.

Variation

This version is a quick method for preparing Wattalappam Pudding. Here, in contrast to the smooth texture achieved in the above method (via steaming) the pudding will be more textured.

12 to 14 ounces grated *kithul* jaggery (palm sugar)
10 large eggs
2 cups coconut milk or thick coconut milk (see page 31)
$1/4$ to $1/2$ teaspoon ground cinnamon
$1/4$ teaspoon ground cloves
$1/8$ to $1/4$ teaspoon ground cardamom
Freshly grated nutmeg to taste
Pinch of salt
15 raw cashew nut halves

Make the pudding mixture as above (substituting 6 to 8 large eggs for the 10), and place the blended pudding mixture in a medium bowl. The total microwave cooking time (on high power) is 12 to 15 minutes. Microwave first for 2 minutes, add the cashew nuts and cook for another 3 minutes. Continue to cook 1 to 2 minutes at a time (for 6 minutes), and then for 30 seconds at a time until ready. After each cooking, examine the pudding for doneness. When ready the pudding should be cooked through and firm to the touch with the center slightly wobbly. Cool to room temperature, cover, and refrigerate for 6 to 8 hours.

Mango Fantasy

Serves 6 to 8

Delightfully delicious and light, this exotic pudding is a mango lover's dream come true. This quick and simple recipe is unique, refreshing, and adventurous.

Place the unopened can of evaporated milk in a pot of boiling water and boil for 10 to 15 minutes. Cool to room temperature and freeze for 1 to 2 hours. In a medium bowl, combine the evaporated milk and cream of tartar. Whisk until it approximately doubles in volume.

In a small bowl combine the gelatin with 3 tablespoon of water. Set aside. To the yolks, add the sugar and mango pulp. Place over a pot of simmering water and whisk continuously for approximately 8 minutes until thickened (streaky stage).

Take off heat and whisk in the gelatin, cinnamon, lime zest, orange zest if using, and season with lime juice. Carefully fold in the whisked evaporated milk and coconut. Ensure the ingredients are evenly incorporated. Transfer to a serving dish, cover, and refrigerate until set and chilled. (For best results refrigerate for 6 hours.) This mango pudding is tremendous served either with a rich dark chocolate sauce or dark chocolate ice cream.

1 (12-ounce) can evaporated milk
1/4 teaspoon cream of tartar
2 level teaspoons gelatin
2 large egg yolks, beaten
3 tablespoons sugar
1/2 cup mango pulp
Pinch of ground cinnamon
1/8 teaspoon lime zest
1/2 teaspoon orange zest (optional)
Fresh lime juice to taste
1 to 2 tablespoons sweetened coconut flakes or shavings.

Banana Fritters with Treacle and Coconut Milk

Serves 4 to 6

This fun dessert is an absolute banana bonanza, where the delicate banana fritters are complemented by the exotic combination of treacle, coconut milk, and spice.

In a medium bowl combine the flour, baking powder, sugar, and salt. Mix well and add the milk and egg. Whisk to form the batter.

Peel and cut the bananas into approximately 3 by 1-inch fingers. Transfer the banana fingers to the batter.

Heat the oil in a medium saucepan. Fry the batter dipped bananas in batches until golden brown. Drain the excess oil on plenty of absorbent paper. Sprinkle the cinnamon, cocoa powder, and powdered sugar over the fried fritters.

When ready to serve (best served warm), place 5 to 6 fritters per portion on a plate. Carefully drizzle approximately 2 teaspoons each of the treacle and coconut milk over the fritters.

Variation
For a more exotic difference, substitute lightly pan-roasted white rice flour for the all-purpose flour and thick coconut milk (see page 31) for the 2% milk.

1 cup all-purpose flour
1/4 teaspoon baking powder
1 tablespoon sugar
Pinch of salt
1 cup cold 2% milk
1 large egg
4 moderately ripe large
   bananas
Oil for deep-frying
1/4 teaspoon ground
   cinnamon
1/2 teaspoon cocoa powder
1 teaspoon powdered sugar
1/3 cup *kithul* treacle or dark
   golden syrup
1/3 cup canned coconut milk,
   warmed though

Broeder

This dough cake of Dutch origin is particularly popular in Sri Lanka at teatime and during the festive season. This variation incorporates dark brown sugar and a bouquet of aromatic spices.

In a medium bowl combine the yeast, sugar, and milk. Mix well and make certain the yeast is well mixed with the milk. Set aside. It is imperative that the milk is warm but not hot, as it will otherwise kill the yeast.

In a medium bowl combine the flour and salt. Mix well to evenly distribute the salt. Add the yeast mixture into the center of the flour and mix lightly. Gradually add the water to form a soft dough. Form into a ball. Place the dough in a well greased medium bowl (use approximately ¾ table-spoon oil), loosely cover with plastic wrap, and let it stand in a warm place for approximately 15 minutes.

Turn the dough onto a lightly floured surface and knead thoroughly (pushing and pulling and adding a little flour if necessary) for about 7 minutes. Add approximately 1 tablespoon oil in the same bowl, lightly grease the bowl, place the dough, and turn the dough over once to coat with oil. Loosely cover with plastic wrap and leave in a warm place for another 20 minutes.

Preheat the oven to 325°F. Prepare a 9 or 9½-inch fluted tube nonstick cake pan by greasing well with butter. In a small bowl combine the butter, sugar, cinnamon, cardamom, cloves if using, and nutmeg. Mix to evenly distribute the ingredients. To the dough add the bicarbonate mixture and sugar mixture. Mix well until thoroughly incorporated. Gradually add the egg yolks and mix thoroughly until fully incorporated and a thick batter is formed.

Evenly place ⅓ cup raisins at the base and sides of the greased baking tin. Add about ⅔ cup raisins to the dough batter, mix well, and carefully transfer to the prepared tin. Evenly sprinkle the remaining raisins, cover with plastic wrap, and leave in a warm place for approximately 20 minutes. Position on the center rack and bake for approximately 45 minutes, until golden in color and an inserted toothpick comes out clean. Turn the cake out and place it inverted on a rack or plate. Let rest for a few minutes before serving. This cake can be presented dusted with powdered sugar and is delicious served with butter.

¾ teaspoon active dry yeast
½ teaspoon sugar
1 cup warm 2% milk
4 cups all-purpose flour
1 to 1½ teaspoons salt
¾ cup warm water
8 tablespoons butter, at
    room temperature
1½ cups dark brown sugar
¼ to ½ teaspoon ground
    cinnamon
¼ teaspoon ground
    cardamom
¼ teaspoon ground cloves
    (optional)
¼ teaspoon freshly grated
    nutmeg
⅔ teaspoon bicarbonate
    of soda mixed with
    1 teaspoon milk
12 large egg yolks, beaten,
    at room temperature
1⅓ cups dark raisins

Payasum

This beautiful semolina-based Tamil dessert combines a medley of both exotic and basic flavors. Frying of the cashews, raisins, and semolina in ghee introduces a new depth of flavor and texture to this classic dish.

In a medium nonstick saucepan combine the ghee and cashews and fry until golden brown. Stir frequently to prevent burning. Drain on absorbent paper. Fry the raisins for a few seconds in the same ghee and drain the excess oil on absorbent paper.

Add the semolina to the same ghee and fry on low heat until golden brown. Stir constantly to prevent burning. Stir in the water and simmer on moderately low heat for approximately 5 minutes. Add the milk and boil up on high heat, take off heat and stir down (by stirring constantly), return to heat and boil up again. Repeat this process 5 times.

Stir in the sugar, cardamom, clove, and rose essence if using. Let cool completely to room temperature. Stir frequently during cooling. Typically, Payasum takes on a rather runny consistency. Prior to serving stir in the cashew nuts and raisins. This dish could be served either cooled to room temperature or slightly chilled.

2 to 2 1/2 tablespoons ghee
15 to 20 cashew nuts,
  roughly chopped
1 tablespoon raisins
1/4 cup semolina
1 1/2 cups boiling water
2 cups warm whole milk
Sugar to taste (approximately
  3 tablespoons
  recommended)
1/8 teaspoon ground
  cardamom
Pinch of ground cloves
1 to 2 drops rose essence
  (optional)

Variation
For a delightful difference in flavor, substitute warm coconut milk for 1/2 cup milk.

Stewed Rhubarb with Custard Sauce

Serves 4

Creating an appealing union, the inherent tart flavor and attractive hue of rhubarb is complemented by the creamy coconut custard sauce.

If coarse, peel the rhubarb stalks lengthwise in order to get rid of the tough undesirable fibers. Wash and cut into approximately 1-inch lengths. (If the stalks are over 1½ inches wide, cut in 2 lengthwise first and then cut across.)

In a moderately small nonstick saucepan combine the rhubarb and the sugar minus 1 tablespoon and set aside for about 20 minutes. Add ⅓ to ½ cup water, bring to a boil, and cook on moderately high heat for approximately 5 minutes, until the rhubarb is tender. When ready the rhubarb should retain its shape and a syrup should be formed. Stir frequently and add a little water if necessary. Stir in the food color. Let cool without stirring and refrigerate until chilled.

1 pound rhubarb stalks
1¼ cups sugar
1 to 2 drops red food color
3 large egg yolks
1 cup thick coconut milk
  (see page 31)
Seeds of 1 small vanilla bean
  or 1 to 2 drops vanilla
  extract

To make the custard sauce: In a small bowl combine the egg yolks and remaining 1 tablespoon sugar and whisk until slightly thickened. Combine the coconut milk and vanilla seeds or extracts in a small saucepan and cook on medium heat until small bubbles begin to barely break the surface. Stir constantly. Gradually add the milk to the egg mixture and whisk constantly. Return the mixture to the saucepan and cook on moderately low heat until slightly thickened. Take off heat and stir constantly for about 3 minutes. Pass through a sieve into a small bowl and let cool to room temperature. Stir occasionally during this time to prevent a skin from forming. The sauce will continue to thicken. Cover and refrigerate until chilled, stirring occasionally. Spoon over the stewed rhubarb and serve.

Jaggery Cake

The essence of this rich cake is a bouquet of exotic and tremendously flavorful ingredients and their unique flavors reminiscent of Sri Lanka.

Pan-roast the semolina on moderate heat for 1 to 2 minutes until very slightly roasted (warmed through and not colored). Stir constantly to prevent burning. Preheat the oven to 250°F.

In a medium bowl combine the sugar, egg yolks, and butter. Beat to a cream and stir in the rose water and essence. Beat for another few seconds. In a clean dry bowl whisk the egg whites together with cream of tartar if using to a soft peak state.

1 cup semolina
$1/2$ cup sugar
3 large eggs, separated,
   at room temperature
6 tablespoons unsalted
   butter, at room temperature
$1/8$ cup rose water
2 to 3 drops rose essence or
   vanilla extract
Pinch of cream of tartar
   (optional)
1 cup finely grated *kithul*
   jaggery (palm sugar)
$1/2$ teaspoon baking powder
$1/4$ teaspoon ground cloves
$1/4$ teaspoon freshly grated
   nutmeg
$1/4$ teaspoon ground
   cinnamon
$1/3$ to $1/2$ cup chopped
   cashew nuts
$1/2$ cup canned coconut milk

To the creamed ingredients stir in the jaggery, semolina, baking powder, clove, nutmeg, cinnamon, and cashew nuts. Stir well to evenly distribute all the ingredients and carefully fold in the egg whites. Ensure the whites are well incorporated into the batter. Gradually mix in the coconut milk.

Pour the batter into a well greased approximately 8 by 8 by 2-inch square nonstick cake pan, position on the center rack, and bake for approximately 1 hour 20 minutes. When ready a toothpick inserted in the center should come out clean. Jaggery Cake is delicious served either warm or at room temperature.

SWEETMEATS

Sri Lankan sweetmeats are popularly known as *kavili* or *rasa kavili*.
A parasol to a vast repertoire of recipes, these delicious traditional candies
are commonly served during the Sinhala-Tamil New Year season and
often on other special occasions such as weddings. *Kavili* also make
a welcome teatime treat. *Kavum*, *Kokis*, *Aggala*, and *Bibikkan* are just
a few of the mouthwatering recipes included in this section.
Most of these unique culinary works of art are, prepared in advance with
much tender loving care. These recipes often call for exotic key ingredients
such as *kithul* treacle, jaggery, semolina, and cashew nuts.
Traditionally, an added depth of flavor is introduced by the use of coconut
oil when a recipe calls for the deep-frying of a sweetmeat.

Aluva

*A*luva are traditionally diamond-shaped delectable sweets that are guaranteed to melt in your mouth. Here is a beautiful convergence of simple ingredients to achieve a heightened result.

Pan-roast the flour on moderate heat for approximately 10 minutes. Stir constantly to prevent burning. Separately pan-roast the cumin and finely grind.

In a moderately small nonstick saucepan, combine the sugar with 1/2 cup water. Bring to a boil and cook on moderate heat for approximately 3 minutes. If using an open flame it is best to use a heat dissipater to ensure even cooking. Add 1 1/2 cups rice flour, cashews, essence, and butter. Stir briskly and constantly for 30 to 40 seconds to form a smooth paste. Avoid overcooking the flour, as it will result in a sticky *aluva* mixture.

1 3/4 cups white rice flour
1/4 teaspoon cumin seeds
3/4 cup sugar
25 whole cashews, roughly
   chopped
2 to 3 drops rose essence
1 teaspoon butter

Lightly flour a board with a portion of the remaining rice flour and turn the aluva mixture on to the board. Kneading with the hand, flatten out the mixture to form an approximately 1/2-inch-thick layer. (It is best to shape into a large diamond to eliminate wastage when cutting.) Sprinkle the top to coat with the remaining flour and cut into diamond-shaped pieces.

Athiraha

The exotic flavor of *kithul* treacle and the beautiful nutty flavor and unique texture of the roasted semolina combine perfectly with rice flour to yield this appetizing fried treat.

Gently pan-roast the semolina until it turns a golden brown color. Stir constantly to prevent burning.

Combine the treacle and salt in an approximately 6-inch nonstick saucepan. On high heat bring to a boil. Take off the heat and briskly stir in the flour and semolina. Stir continuously to form a smooth paste. Transfer the mixture to a plate and let cool completely to room temperature.

1 tablespoon semolina
1/2 cup *kithul* treacle
Pinch of salt
1 cup rice flour
Oil for deep-frying

Add 1 cup water to the same saucepan and stir over a high heat for 2 to 3 minutes, until a slightly thickened broth is formed. (The water thickens into a broth based on any mixture stuck to the saucepan and this step is followed so as not to waste any of the flavor.) Since we are using a nonstick saucepan the broth may not form and in this instance it is perfectly acceptable to use the non-broth-water, cooled to room temperature. Set aside and let cool completely.

With the hand, knead the cooled *athiraha* mixture thoroughly. Add the broth as needed in order to soften the mixture sufficiently to form balls. Form the mixture into 15 balls and flatten each on an oiled surface (lightly grease the hands) into rounds.

Deep-fry on moderately high heat until dark brown in color. Take care not to burn the *athiraha*. Drain the excess oil on plenty of absorbent paper. Cool completely to room temperature before serving. This sweetmeat will keep for 2 weeks stored in an airtight container at room temperature.

Bibikkan

25 servings

*B*ibikkan is best introduced as a luscious slowly cooked rich coconut cake. In this authentic recipe a seductive blend of exotic ingredients complements the unifying flavor of coconut.

In a medium bowl combine the coconut and treacle. Mix well to evenly distribute the ingredients. In a medium nonstick saucepan, combine the sugar with 1 cup water. Stir once and cook on high heat until the sugar syrup turns pale golden. Stirring constantly cook for another few seconds until it turns a deep golden brown (caramel) hue.

Briskly stir in the coconut mixture and cook on moderate heat for approximately 5 minutes. Stir frequently. Season this *pani pol* mixture with salt and stir in the cumin, nutmeg, cardamom, and clove. Set aside to cool to room temperature.

Preheat the oven to 250°F. Liberally grease an approximately 8 by 8 by 2-inch nonstick baking tin with butter. To the cooled *pani pol* add the cashews, lime rind, ginger preserve, melon preserve, dates, raisins, and egg if using. Mix well to evenly distribute the ingredients. In a small bowl mix the flour and baking powder. Add this mixture to the other ingredients and mix to form a heavy batter. If too dry, add a little (up to 1/3 cup) water to slightly loosen the mixture.

Transfer the *bibikkan* batter to the prepared tin and smooth out. (The surface should be smooth, if coconut pieces stand out they tend to burn.) Position on the center rack and bake for approximately 2 hours, until it is a dark golden brown and a toothpick inserted in the center comes out clean. Cool to room temperature before serving. The intermingling flavors unify and the recipe improves over time.

3 cups finely grated fresh or rehydrated desiccated coconut
3/4 cup *kithul* treacle
1 cup sugar
Pinch of salt
1 teaspoon pan-roasted, ground cumin
Pinch of freshly ground nutmeg
Pinch of ground cardamom
Pinch of ground cloves
1/2 cup chopped cashew nuts
Zest of 1 to 2 large limes, finely grated
1 to 1 1/2 tablespoons finely chopped ginger preserve
1 tablespoon finely chopped melon preserve
8 to 10 large dates, finely chopped
1/3 cup (approximately 1 1/2 ounces) raisins
1 large egg, well beaten (optional)
1 cup all-purpose flour
3/4 teaspoon baking powder

Kalu Dodol

Characteristically dark in color and exquisitely rich in flavor, *Kalu Dodol* makes a beautiful accompaniment to a hot cup of freshly brewed tea.

In a moderately small nonstick saucepan, combine the coconut milk, jaggery, and flour. Bring to a boil and stir to dissolve and blend the ingredients. Cook on low heat for 4 to 5 minutes. Stir constantly to prevent burning.

Add the oil and cook on moderate heat for approximately 8 minutes. Stir continuously. The thickening mixture will absorb the oil.

Add the cardamom, cloves, cashews, and salt. Cook for approximately another 2 minutes on moderately low heat. The mixture will begin to release some oil and fry in it. Stir constantly. Carefully scoop out and discard some of the oil. Cook on very low heat for approximately 15 minutes and stir continuously. When ready, the mixture should be dark in color, unified, and almost set. It should not be sticky and toffee-like.

1$\frac{1}{2}$ cups canned coconut milk
8 ounces *kithul* jaggery (palm sugar), grated
2 ounces rice flour
$\frac{1}{2}$ cup vegetable oil
$\frac{1}{8}$ teaspoon ground cardamom
Pinch of ground cloves
$\frac{1}{3}$ cup roughly chopped
Pinch of salt

Transfer to an approximately 10-inch nonstick loaf tin rinsed with cold water. Smooth out to form an even layer. Pour out any remaining oil by carefully tilting the tin) and let cool to room temperature. For best results leave for 24 hours, transfer to a airtight container lined with oil paper, and leave for another 8 to 12 hours for flavors and texture to develop. Cut the *kalu dodol* into pieces when ready to serve.

Moong Kavum

Makes 15 to 20

Moong Kavum are batter-fried, sweet, and tantalizing creations that combine the unique flavors of green gram, *kithul* treacle, ghee, and coconut.

To prepare the moong flour for this recipe pan-roast moong dhal (husked and split) on moderate heat for approximately 10 minutes, until golden brown. Stir constantly to ensure even cooking and to prevent burning. Grind to a powder and sift. Alternatively pan-roast the moong flour on moderate heat for 8 to 10 minutes (until slightly colored) and sift. Stir constantly to prevent burning.

Combine the treacle and pinch of salt in an approximately 6-inch nonstick saucepan. Bring to a boil on high heat. Take off the heat and briskly stir in the moong flour, $1/2$-cup rice flour, and ghee. Transfer on to a board and cool to room temperature.

Add 1 cup water to the same saucepan and return to heat. Stirring constantly cook on moderately high heat for approximately 1 minute, until a slightly thick broth is formed. Take off heat and let cool completely. (The water thickens into a broth based on any mixture stuck to the saucepan, so as not to waste any flavor. Since we are using a nonstick saucepan the broth may not form and in this instance it is perfectly acceptable to use the non-broth water, cooled to room temperature.)

- $1/2$ cup moong (green gram) flour
- $1/2$ cup *kithul* treacle
- Pinch of salt
- $1 1/4$ cup rice flour
- $3/4$ teaspoon ghee or butter
- Salt to taste
- 1 cup water or coconut milk
- Pinch to $1/8$ teaspoon ground saffron or turmeric powder
- Oil for deep-frying

Adding the broth as necessary in order to loosen the cooled mixture, knead by hand until crack free. Flatten and smooth the mixture to form an approximately $1/4$- to $1/3$-inch-thick layer and cut into diamond-shaped pieces. A greased piece of baking paper (or traditionally banana leaf) can be used to smooth the flattened mixture.

Make the batter by combining the remaining flour and $3/4$ cup water and seasoning with salt and saffron. Mix well. Heat the oil, carefully dip the diamond shapes in the batter, and deep-fry on moderate heat until golden brown. (As the rice flour tends to sediment, ensure even consistency of the batter by stirring it frequently.) Drain the excess oil on plenty of absorbent paper. Prior to serving cool to room temperature.

Moong Guli

Moong Guli or green gram balls are twice-cooked sweetmeats that incorporate sugar candy in its preparation.

To prepare the moong flour for this recipe pan-roast moong dhal (husked and split) on moderate heat for approximately 10 minutes, until golden brown. Stir constantly to ensure even cooking and to prevent burning. Grind to a powder and sieve. (For the success of this recipe it is imperative that the moong flour is par-cooked otherwise it will result in a raw tasting sweetmeat.)

In an approximately 6-inch nonstick saucepan combine the treacle and salt. Bring to a boil on high heat. Take off the heat and quickly mix in the moong flour, roasted rice flour, and sugar candy. While still warm, quickly form portions of the mixture into bite-size balls. To avoid the balls from crumbling apart it is imperative that they are formed while the mixture is still warm.

Make the batter in a small bowl by combining the remaining rice flour with 1/3 cup water. Mix well and season with salt and saffron.

1/2 cup moong flour
1/4 cup rice flour, pan-roasted until slightly colored
1/2 cup (approximately 4 ounces) ground sugar candy
1/4 cup *kithul* treacle
Pinch of salt
1/3 cup rice flour
Pinch of ground saffron or turmeric powder
Oil for deep-frying

Heat the oil. Dip the balls in the batter and without overcrowding the pan deep-fry until golden brown. (As the rice flour tends to sediment, ensure even consistency of the batter by stirring it frequently.) Drain the excess oil on plenty of absorbent paper. Before serving cool to room temperature.

Lavariya

*L*avariya are unique parcels of rice flour-based dough that envelop a heavenly sweet spice-infused coconut and jaggery filling. Here is a sweetmeat that is steamed to perfection and equally delicious served warm, at room temperature, or cold.

In a medium saucepan combine the coconut, jaggery, rice flour, cinnamon, nutmeg, and 1/2 cup of water. Season with salt and cook on low heat for approximately 8 minutes. Stir frequently to prevent burning. The jaggery will melt into the coconut and when ready this rich *pani pol* will have a sticky, smooth, and soft (not hard and toffee-like) consistency and be a deep golden brown hue. Set aside and let rest for a few minutes.

1 cup finely grated coconut
3/4 cup finely grated *kithul* jaggery (palm sugar)
1/4 teaspoon rice flour
1-inch stick cinnamon
Freshly grated nutmeg, to taste
Salt to taste
1 cup steamed rice flour (steamed for an hour and sifted or lightly pan-roasted. Either white, red or a combination of white and red; page 23)
1 1/4 to 1 1/3 cups boiling water

Draw a 4-inch circle on the underside of a small (approximately 6-inch square) piece of parchment paper. Place the flour in a medium bowl and season with salt. Gradually add the water and mix well to form a thick, smooth stringhopper paste.

Fill a stringhopper apparatus and pour, as described in the recipe for Stringhoppers (page 89), onto the underside of the parchment paper and fill the drawn circle. Carefully place a small portion of the pani pol to cover half the stringhopper, gently lifting the parchment paper fold the other half over to cover the filling. Seal by gently pressing the edges together.

Carefully transfer the delicate *lavariya* onto a lightly greased stringhopper mold or steamer rack. Repeat the pouring, filling, folding, sealing, and transferring until all the mixture is used. Steam the lavariya for approximately 8 minutes until cooked. Let cool a few minutes before serving.

Variation

This *lavariya* preparation is a simpler alternative to the above Stringhopper Lavariya. Take portions of the stringhopper paste and form into balls the size of a small lime. On a greased flat surface flatten the balls into rounds. Place a small portion of the pani pol to cover half the round, carefully fold the other half over, and seal the edges by pressing together. Steam for approximately 8 minutes until cooked. For this version the *pani pol* can be substituted by a simple filling made by mixing equal amounts of rehydrated desiccated coconut and sugar.

Kokis

The essence of this humble recipe lies in its distinctive crispy crunch and authentic flavor. Wonderfully quick and simple to prepare, *Kokis* is guaranteed to leave you craving for more.

In a medium bowl combine the rice flour, bread flour, sugar, and salt. Mix well and gradually add the coconut milk and $\frac{1}{2}$ cup water. Stir in the egg and stir well to make a smooth batter. Adjust salt.

Heat the oil and dip the head of a seasoned *kokis* mold (which comes in attractive shapes like flowers or stars) in the hot oil. This helps condition the mold for baking the *kokis*. Dip the hot mold in the batter being careful not to let the batter coat over $\frac{3}{4}$ way up the mold. Immerse the batter-coated mold in the hot oil and fry on moderate heat for 5 to 8 seconds. During this time help slip the *kokis* off the mold and release it into the oil by gently shaking the mold and teasing it off with a flat small spoon or rounded knife tip.

1 extra large egg, beaten
$\frac{3}{4}$ cup rice flour
$\frac{1}{4}$ cup bread flour
$\frac{1}{2}$ to 1 teaspoon sugar
Salt to taste
$\frac{1}{2}$ cup coconut milk
Oil for deep-frying

Turn the *kokis* over during frying. When ready the *kokis* (which takes on the shape of its mold) should be golden brown and crispy. Keep in mind that once off the heat the *kokis* continue cooking and coloring for 1 to 2 minutes. As this delicate preparation has a high tendency to burn, temperature control is imperative for its success. Drain the excess oil on plenty of absorbent paper and let cool to room temperature. Kokis can be stored successfully for 1 to 2 weeks in an airtight container.

Variation

For a sweet difference sprinkle powdered sugar while the *kokis* is still warm. Alternatively, drizzle a sugar syrup made by a combination of 1 cup sugar and ½ cup water. Cook in a small nonstick saucepan (stirring constantly) on moderately high heat until thickened.

Tip

To season a *kokis* mold, keep its head submerged in hot oil (with the heat on) for 5 to 6 minutes. Then dip in batter and fry the kokis. The first 2 or so may stick to the mold. Remove the stuck pieces and repeat. Once the *kokis* come off (with gentle teasing) the mold is considered seasoned.

Thala Guli

Makes 16

*T*hala Guli, or sesame balls, are also commonly referred to as *Thala Bola*. With each bite of this delicacy one savors the perfect blend of sesame and jaggery.

It is imperative for the success of this recipe that hands and all utensils are completely dry. Place ²/₃ cup sesame seeds in a mortar, add a pinch of salt, and using a pestle grind to crush the seeds.

Leaving approximately 1 tablespoon of the uncrushed sesame seeds aside, combine in a food processor the remaining sesame seeds, crushed sesame seeds, jaggery, and a pinch of salt. (Traditionally, all the ingredients are pounded together in a mortar.) Pulse for a few seconds on low speed and grind on high speed for 1 to 2 minutes until thoroughly blended and a slightly oily paste is formed.

1⅓ cups white (unwashed) sesame seeds
Pinch of salt
8 ounces *kithul* jaggery (palm sugar), grated or broken into small pieces

Transfer the mixture into a medium bowl and mix in the remaining sesame seeds. Knead well (by hand) to evenly distribute the sesame seeds and to form a stiff paste.

Take small portions of the mixture and squeezing tightly between the fingers and palm (and rolling between the palms) form each portion into firm balls or approximately 2-inch long cylindrical shapes. For presentation individually wrap the *thala guli* in decorative oilpaper that has been cut to size. Twist the ends like a toffee wrapper.

Aggala

The hint of peppery bite contributes a fascinating twist to this all-time favorite sweetmeat.

To prepare the rice flour, pan-roast the rice on moderate heat (stir continuously to ensure even cooking) for 8 to 10 minutes until a rich golden brown. Finely grind (best use an electric grinder) and sift through a fine meshed sieve. Regrind and sift the remainder, repeating this process a few times until only about a teaspoonful of coarsely ground rice is left in the sieve. Discard this remainder.

In an approximately 6-inch nonstick saucepan combine the treacle and salt. Bring to a boil (bubble state) on high heat. Immediately take off the heat and stir in $^3/_4$ cup roasted rice flour, pepper, and ginger if using. Mix thoroughly to form a stiff paste.

While still warm, take portions of the paste and form into bite-size balls. Coat the balls well in the remaining flour. Let cool to room temperature before serving.

1 cup basmati rice (other white rice varieties can also be used)
$^1/_2$ cup *kithul* treacle
Pinch of salt
2 to 3 pinches freshly milled black pepper
Pinch of ginger powder (optional)

Variation
For a delightful difference in texture and flavor increase the quantity of *kithul* treacle by approximately 1 teaspoon and mix 1 tablespoon rehydrated desiccated coconut together with the other ingredients.

Tip
Large quantities of rice flour can be prepared in advance to the above method and kept ready at hand.

Stringhopper Asmi

Here is a beautifully delicate sweetmeat that is has a unique crunch and flavor. This recipe is also an inventive method to utilize leftover stringhoppers.

Sun-dry the stringhoppers until completely dehydrated and stiff. Alternatively dry in a warm oven.

In a small nonstick saucepan combine the sugar with ½ cup water. Cook, stirring constantly, until it thickens and forms a syrup. Add the essence and food color and mix well.

Heat the oil and deep-fry the dried stringhoppers until golden and crisp. The dry stringhoppers will swell up beautifully during frying. Turn over during frying. Drain the excess oil on plenty of absorbent paper. Drizzle the sugar syrup in a zigzag pattern over the *asmi*.

15 rice flour stringhoppers
  (page 89)
1 cup sugar
1 to 2 drops rose essence
Pink food color
Oil for deep-frying

Tip

The sun-dried stringhoppers can be successfully stored for 2 to 3 weeks in an airtight container and deep-fried and drizzled with syrup as necessary.

210   **Exotic Tastes of Sri Lanka**

Jaggery Milk Toffee

25 servings

Here is a toffee that combines the sweet goodness of jaggery, delicate flavors of coconut, and refreshing essence of cardamom and vanilla. Cashew nuts introduce both a depth of texture and flavor to this gorgeous candy.

Liberally grease a flat shallow dish or board with butter. In a moderately small nonstick saucepan combine the sugar, jaggery, coconut milk, and condensed milk. Bring to a boil and while warming stir to dissolve the sugar and jaggery.

Cook on moderate heat for approximately 15 minutes and stir constantly to prevent burning. The mixture should thicken considerably. Reduce heat to moderately low and cook for approximately 10 minutes. Add the cashew nuts, vanilla extract, and cardamom. Stir constantly to prevent burning. When ready the movement of the spoon will leave tracks (for a few seconds) in the mixture.

Pour the thickened mixture into the dish or onto the board. Using a greased piece of parchment paper and a spoon carefully and briskly flatten to form a $1/3$ to $1/2$-inch-thick layer. With the tip of a knife (avoid dragging the knife) gently score the surface to mark the square pieces. As the toffee cools keep remarking and pressing down until once cooled the pieces would be cut out.

$1^1/4$ cup sugar
$1/4$ cup finely grated *kithul* jaggery (palm sugar)
1 cup coconut milk
1 (14-ounce) can sweetened condensed milk
$1/4$ cup roughly chopped cashew nuts
2 to 3 drops vanilla extract
$1/8$ to $1/4$ teaspoon ground cardamom

Boroa

Of Portuguese origin, *Boroa* is a delicious dry cookie that successfully pairs the flavors and textures of cashews, semolina, and coconut with rose water. An absolute favorite of mine, *Boroa* are especially popular in southern Sri Lanka.

Preheat the oven to 250°F. In a medium bowl combine the semolina, sugar, and coconut. Mix well to evenly distribute the ingredients. Stir in the egg and rose water. Mix for a few minutes and form into a crumbly paste.

Divide the mixture into 9 and form each portion into balls. On a baking tray lined with parchment paper flatten the balls into approximately 1/3-inch-thick rounds. Ensure to leave enough space between the cookies. If using, stud each round with a cashew nut half.

1/2 cup semolina
1/2 cup sugar
1/2 cup desiccated coconut
1 large egg, beaten, at room
   temperature
1/8 cup rose water
9 cashew nut halves (optional)

Place the tray on the center rack and bake for approximately 1 hour 20 minutes, until golden brown. (For a softer, slightly chewy cookie remove from oven 5 to 10 minutes earlier.) Let cool to room temperature.

Laddu

This mouthwatering sweet-meat is amazingly simple to prepare and is guaranteed to melt in the mouth. *Laddu* is a perfect combination of roasted rice flour, coconut, and sugar.

To prepare the rice flour, pan-roast the rice on moderate heat (stir continuously to ensure even cooking) for 8 to 10 minutes until a rich golden brown. Finely grind (best use an electric grinder) and sift through a fine meshed sieve. Regrind and sift the remainder, repeating this process a few times until only about a teaspoonful of coarsely ground rice is left in the sieve. Discard this remainder.

In a medium bowl combine the coconut, sugar, and salt. Using a fork mix well to evenly distribute the ingredients. Add 1 cup roasted rice flour and mix well to evenly distribute the ingredients.

Gradually add the water and stir constantly. If the mixture is too dry, add a few drops of boiling water as necessary. While still warm take portions of the mixture and form into balls. Coat the balls well in the remaining rice flour. Cool to room temperature before serving. The traditional recipe for *Laddu* calls for freshly grated coconut but I prefer to use desiccated coconut.

1^1/4 cups basmati rice
  (other white rice varieties
  could be used)
^{1}/2 cup desiccated coconut,
  rehydrated
^{1}/2 cup sugar
Pinch of salt
^{1}/3 cup boiling water

Coconut Toffee

Pol Toffee

20 servings

Coconut Toffee is a delightful sweet that combines coconut, sugar, and essence of rose to perfection.

In a moderately small nonstick saucepan combine the sugar with ½ cup water and bring to a boil. Cook on moderate heat for approximately 5 minutes, until thickened. Stir frequently to prevent coloring and caramelizing.

Mix in the coconut and cook on moderate heat for 10 minutes. Stir frequently. Add the essence and food color and cook until thickened for approximately another 10 minutes. Stir frequently.

Transfer to a dish (preferably flat Pyrex square or rectangular) rinsed with cold water and pour the mixture in. Even out the mixture into a flat layer approximately ¾-inch-thick, let cool for approximately 3 minutes, and cut into squares.

2 cups sugar
2 tightly packed cups
  rehydrated desiccated
  coconut or finely grated
  fresh coconut
1 to 2 drops rose essence
1 to 2 drops pink food color

Variation

One small boiled, peeled, and mashed potato can be added to the mixture at the halfway cooking point. It introduces a new dimension of texture and flavor.

Naran Kavum

This authentic Sri Lankan sweetmeat with a distinct flavor and texture is guaranteed to delight the taste buds.

In a medium saucepan combine the coconut, jaggery, rice flour, cinnamon, nutmeg, zest, and 1/2 cup of water. Season with salt and cook on low heat for approximately 8 minutes. Stir frequently to prevent burning. The jaggery will melt into the coconut and when ready this rich *pani pol* will have a sticky, smooth, and soft (not hard and toffee-like) consistency and be a deep golden brown hue. Set aside and let rest for a few minutes.

In a medium bowl combine the roasted rice and water. Mix well to form a stiff paste and season with salt. Make the paste into *pittu* granules as described for *Pittu* (page 88). It is simplest to use either the cutting method or the food processor method. Steam for approximately 5 minutes until cooked. Transfer to a medium bowl and let cool for a few minutes.

While the *pittu* is still warm add 1/2 to 2/3 cups of the *pani pol* and mix well with the hand. Add the all-purpose flour as necessary in order to form the mixture into firm balls.

Make the batter by combining the remaining flour, 1/2 cup cold water, and saffron. Mix well and season with salt. Heat the oil, dip the *kavum* balls in batter, and deep-fry until golden brown. Drain the excess oil on plenty of absorbent paper. Best served at room temperature.

1 cup finely grated coconut
3/4 cup finely grated *kithul* jaggery (palm sugar)
1/4 teaspoon rice flour
1-inch stick cinnamon
Freshly grated nutmeg, to taste
1/8 to 1/4 teaspoon grated zest of mandarin or orange
Salt to taste
1/2 cup roasted rice flour
1/2 cup boiling water
1 to 3 teaspoons all-purpose flour
1/2 cup white rice flour
Pinch to 1/8 teaspoon finely ground saffron or turmeric powder
Oil for deep-frying

Authentic Meals

Though the menu is entirely to your discretion, a few noteworthy points will make your Sri Lankan meal a tremendous success. When combining traditional entrées for a meal, always include one or more mild dishes when serving a spicy hot dish. Further, ensure the entrées complement the overall meal, for certain flavors and textures will work together beautifully while others simply may not. The following recipe groupings are a guide to formulating successful Sri Lankan menus.

White or Red Steamed Rice with:

Karavala Theldala
Coconut Sambol
Dhal Curry
Green Bean Curry
Pappadam

Country-Style Fried Fish
Gotukola Saladé
Tender Jack Fruit Curry
Country Cucumber Curry

Ash Plantain Curry
Coconut Sambol
Maalu Bada Badum
Beetroot Curry

Spicy Chicken Curry
Traditional Eggplant Salad
Dhal (with spinach) Curry
Okra Theldala

Breadfruit Mallum
Karavala Curry
Pappadam

Fish Ambul-Thiyal
White Potato Curry
Karavila Salad
Pappadam
Fried Butter Chilies

Spicy Fish Curry
Thalana Batu Curry
Kale Mallum

Traditional Squid Curry
Coconut Sambol
White Potato Curry
Pappadam

Pork Kalu Pol Curry
Ala Theldala
Gotukola Saladé

Anchovies with Okra and Tamarind
Northern Eggplant Curry
Kale Mallum
Pappadam
Butter Chilies

Traditional Squid Curry
Breadfruit Mallum
Okra Theldala
Cool Cucumber Saladé

Fish Ambul-Thiyal
Mango Curry
Drumstick Curry
Gotukola Saladé

White or Red Steamed Rice with:
Traditional Sri Lankan Crab Curry
Gotukola Saladé or Cool Cucumber Saladé
Pappadam

Special Rice Preparations:
Fragrant Fried Rice
Spicy Chicken Curry
Ala Theldala
Sri Lankan-Style Savory Omelet
Traditional Eggplant Salad

Tamarind Rice
Spicy Baked Chicken
Stuffed Fried Capsicums
Dhal Curry
Cool Cucumber Saladé

Cilantro Rice
Lamb with Tomatoes
Ala Theldala
Savory Fish Cutlets
Cool Cucumber Saladé

Yellow Rice
Fish in a Fried Onion and Tomato
Sauce
Meat-Filled Capsicums
Eggplant Moju

Lamb Buriyani
Authentic Mutton Curry
Mint Sambol
Cool Cucumber Saladé (version
with yogurt)

Rice Pilau
Fish and Mushroom Pie
Dinner Eggs
Spicy Chicken Curry

Fragrant Fried Rice
Baked Crab Delight
Eggplant Moju
Prawns with Onion and Chili
White Potato Curry
Cool Cucumber Saladé

Yellow Rice or Rice Pilau
Stuffed Squid Serenade
Stuffed Capsicum Theldala
Savory Fish Cutlets
Dhal Curry

Fragrant Fried Rice
Piquant Prawn Curry
Eggplant Moju
Ala Theldala
Mint Sambol

Yellow Rice, Fragrant Fried Rice,
or Rice Pilau
Beef and Green Pepper Badum
Coconut Sambol (pan-roasted version)
Stuffed Fried Capsicums
White Potato Curry

Yellow Rice or Fragrant Fried Rice
Cashews with Green Peas and Carrots
Breaded Fried Fish
Eggplant Moju or Traditional
Eggplant Salad
Spicy Chicken Curry
Dhal Curry

Special Rice Preparations:
Milk Rice
Seeni Sambol, Luni Miris, or *Katta
Sambol*, and/or Mango Curry

Milk Rice
Fish Ambul-Thiyal,
Spicy Chicken Curry, Spicy Fish
Curry, or Authentic Mutton Curry

Stringhoppers or Stringhopper Pilau with:
Fried Egg Curry or White Fish
Curry
Coconut Sambol

White Potato Curry
Fish Ambul-Thiyal
Coconut Sambol

Seeni Sambol
White Potato Curry or White Fish
Curry
Mango Curry

Spicy Chicken Curry or Spicy Fish
Curry
Coconut Mallum

Authentic Mutton Curry or Spicy
Beef and Potato Curry
Prawn Sambol
Ala Theldala
Eggplant Moju

White Mutton Curry
Coconut Sambol or *Seeni Sambol*

Fish in a Fried Onion and Tomato
Sauce
White Potato Curry
Prawn Sambol
Eggplant Moju

Thosai or Idly with:
Chicken with Cilantro and Tomato
Coconut Sambol
Sambar

Spicy Chicken Curry or Authentic
Mutton Curry
Mint Sambol
Ala Theldala

Coconut Sambol
Eggplant Moju
Sambar

Hoppers (Plain and Egg) with:
Spicy Fish Curry or Spicy Chicken
Curry
Katta Sambol or *Lunu Miris*
Butter

Piquant Prawn Curry
Authentic Mutton Curry or Pork
Kalu Pol Curry
Ala Theldala
Seeni Sambol or Coconut Sambol
Butter

Pittu with:
Katta Sambol or *Lunu Miris*
Coconut Milk (slightly warmed)

Ripe Mango or Banana (as a
dessert)
Authentic Mutton Curry
Ala Theldala

Coconut Roti with:
Spicy Fish Curry or Spicy Chicken
Curry
Katta Sambol or *Lunu Miris*
Butter

Authentic Mutton Curry or Spicy
Beef and Potato Curry
Lunu Miris

Jam
Butter

Mild Dishes

Sri Lankan cuisine offers an array of mild dishes that are delicious on their own and equally satisfying when complementing an overall hot and spicy menu. The majority of the other recipes can also be modified to a milder heat by simply reducing the amount of chili (whole [fresh or dry], powder, flakes, curry powders, etc.) to taste. The majority of staples are considered mild.

Anchovies with Okra and Tamarind
Ash Plantain Curry
Baked Crab Delight
Batter-Fried Anchovies
Batter-Fried Chicken
Breaded Fried Fish
Breadfruit Mallum
Cabbage Mallum
Cashews with Green Peas and Carrots
Coconut Mallum
Cool Cucumber Saladé
Country Cucumber Curry
Country-Style Fried Fish
Crispy Bitter Gourd Salad
Crunchy Carrot Saladé
Dinner Eggs
Drumstick Curry
Fish in a Fried Onion and Tomato
    Sauce
Fish Sauté
Fried Egg Curry
Gotukola Saladé
Green Bean Curry
Liver Curry
Mackerel Salad
Meat-Filled Capsicums
Moong Dhal Curry
Northern Eggplant Curry
Pineapple-Cheese-Liver-Onion Sticks
Prawn Vadai

Prawns Wrapped in Spicy Pastry
Sassy Egg Salad
Snake Gourd Curry
Sri Lankan-Style Chicken Stew
Sri Lankan-Style Savory Omelet
Thatta Vadai
Traditional Dhal Curry
Traditional Eggplant Salad
Ulunthu Vadai
Vegetable Rainbow Salad
Vegetable Sandwiches
White Chicken Curry
White Fish Curry
White Lamb Curry
White Mutton Curry
White Potato Curry
Wild Eggplant Curry
Zucchini Curry

Index

(Recipe* refers to the variation(s) of that recipe)
(Recipe' refers to tip(s) for that recipe)

A

Ambul-thiyal,
  about, 11
  with eggplant, see eggplant moju*, 98
  fish, 168
Anchovies,
  about, 16
  batter fried, 50
  with okra and tamarind (*nethali theeyel*), 166
  see dry fish
  also see fish
Appetizers, 33-52
  anchovies, batter fried, 50
  capsicums,
    meat filled, 40
    stuffed fried, 37
  chicken patties, 34
  chickpeas, with coconut, stir-fried, 48
  cocktail sticks (pineapple-cheese-liver-onion), 52
  eggs, dinner, 136
  fish buns (*maalu paan*), 44
  fish, country style fried, 173
  fish cutlets, savory, 36
  fish rolls, see mutton rolls*, 42
  minced beef pastries, 47
  mutton rolls, 42
  potato balls (*ala bola*), 41
  seeni sambol buns, see fish buns*, 44
  stuffed godamba roti, 46
  prawn vadai, 154
  prawns wrapped in spicy pastry, 51
  vadai
    chana, see prawn vadai*, 154
    prawn, 154
    thatta, 39
    ulunthu vadai, 38

Appetizers, continued
  vegetable sandwiches, 49
Ash plantain(s)
  about, 24
  curry, 107
Avocado pudding, 180

B

Badum, about, 11
Banana(s)
  fritters with treacle and coconut milk, 191
  in fruit salad, see tropical fruit salad, 182
Beef
  deviled, 139
  dinner eggs, 136
  and green pepper badum, 138
  liver curry, 140
  meat filled capsicums, 40
  minced meat with cauliflower and onion, 144
  minced, pastries, 47
  and potato curry, spicy, 137
Beetroot
  curry, 100
  see vegetable rainbow salad, 55
  also see vegetable sandwiches, 49
Bitter gourd (*karavila*)
  about, 25-26
  salad, crispy, 57
  with tomatoes, 105
Breadfruit
  about, 24
  mallum, 56
Butter Chilies (*moru miris*), about, 11

C

Cabbage mallum, 68
Cake
  coconut-honey, see *bibikkan*
  bibikkan (eggless recipe), 200
  broeder, 192
  date, 188
  Dutch dough, see broeder
  jaggery, 196
  pani pol, see *bibikkan*
Capsicum(s)
  about, 12
  badum, stuffed, 106
  chicken with, and tomatoes, 127
  meat filled, 40
  stuffed fried, 37
Carrot(s)
  saladé, crunchy, 62
  see vegetable rainbow salad, 55
  also see vegetable sandwiches, 49
Cashews with green peas and carrots, 101
Cassava
  about, 24-25
  curry, traditional, 115
Cauliflower and onion, minced meat
  with, 144
Chicken
  batter-fried, 132
  with capsicums and tomatoes, 127
  with cilantro and tomatoes, 130
  curry, spicy, 126
  curry, white, see white mutton curry*,
    142
  koththu roti, 94
  livers with onion and chili, 131
  patties, 34
  spicy baked, 129
  stew, Sri Lankan-style, 128
  stringhopper pilau, 90

Chili(es)
  about, 11-13
  butter (*moru miris*), about, 12
  see capsicums
  also see curry powders
  for milder heat, see suggestions, 31
Cilantro, rice, 75
Coconut
  about, 13-14
  chickpeas stir-fried with, 48
  mallum (*pol mallum*), 60
  roti, savory (*pol roti*), 83
  sambol (*pol sambol*), 58
  toffee, 214
  also see kalu pol and *pani pol*
Crab(s)
  baked, delight, 159
  curry, traditional Sri Lankan, 156
  deviled, 158
Crepes, savory,
  traditional thosai, 85
Crepes, sweet,
  honey-coconut, 187
Cucumber
  curry, country, 104
  saladé, cool, 67
  see vegetable rainbow salad, 55
Curry powders, about, 15
Cuttlefish, see squid

D

Date cake, 88
Desserts
  avocado pudding, 180
  banana fritters with treacle and
    coconut milk, 191
  broeder, 192
  caramel pudding, 184
  crepes, honey-coconut, 187
  date cake, 188
  divul kiri, see wood apple cream
  dough cake, see broeder

Desserts, continued
  fritters, banana, with treacle and
    coconut milk, 191
  fruit salad, tropical, 182
  jaggery cake, 196
  mango fantasy, 190
  payasum, 194
  pineapple fluff, 186
  rhubarb, stewed, with custard sauce, 195
  sago pudding, 183
  wattalappam pudding, 189
  wood apple cream (*divul kiri*), 181
  also see Sweetmeats
Dhal(s), *see* Lentils
Drumstick(s) (*murunga*)
  about, 25
  curry, 123'
Dry Fish (*karavala*)
  about, 17-18
  anchovy with eggplant, *see* eggplant
    moju*, 98
  curry, traditional, 174
  theldala, 175

E

Eggplant
  curry, northern (*vellai kathirikkai*), 118
  moju, 98
  salad, traditional, 54
  with prawns, 152
Egg(s)
  curry, fried, 133
  dinner, 136
  fried rice, *see* fragrant fried rice*, 82
  godamba roti, *see godamba roti**, 93
  hoppers, *see* traditional hoppers*, 91
  omelet, Sri Lankan-style savory, 135
  poached, curry, 134
  salad, sassy, 64
  yellow rice with, *see* yellow rice*, 76

F

Fish
  about, 15-16
  ambul-thiyal, 168
  anchovies, batter fried, 50
  anchovies with okra and tamarind
    (*nethali theeyel*), 166
  breaded fried, 171
  buns (*maalu paan*), 44
  curry, spicy, 160
  curry, white, 167
  cutlets, savory, 36
  fried, country-style, 173
  with fried okra, *see* twice-cooked
    fish*, 163
  in a fried onion and tomato sauce, 170
  intestine and roe badum (*maalu-bada
    badum*)169
  karavala, *see* dry fish
  mackerel salad, 70
  and mushroom pie, 164
  patties, *see* chicken patties*, 34
  roe and intestine badum, 169
  rolls, *see* mutton rolls*, 42
  sauté, 172
  stuffed godamba roti, 46
  stuffed fried capsicums, 37
  twice-cooked, 163
  vara, 162
  also see dry fish
Flours, steaming, about, 23
Fruit, salad, tropical, 182

G

Gamboge
  about, 16-17
  see ambul-thiyal
  also incorporated in:
    fish curry, spicy, 160
    jackfruit curry, tender (*polos curry*),
      111
    squid curry, traditional, 176

Ghee, about, 17
Goraka, see gamboge
Gotukola
  about, 25
  saladé, 63
Green bean curry, 121

H
Herbs, about, 21-24

J
Jackfruit
  about, 25
  curry, tender jackfruit (polos achcharu),
    111
  pickle, tender jackfruit (polos curry), 103
Jaggery
  about, 17
  cake, 196
  in desserts and sweetmeats:
    avocado pudding*, 180
    kalu dodol, 201
    lavariya, 204
    naran kavum, 215
    sago pudding, 183
    thala guli, 208
    wattalappam pudding, 189
    wood apple cream, 181
    milk toffee, 211

K
Kale mallum, 71
Kalu Pol
  about, 17
  pork kalu pol curry, 147
  pumpkin kalu pol curry, 112
Karavila, see bitter gourd

L
Lamb
  buriyani, 80
  curry, see authentic mutton curry*, 141

Lamb, continued
  curry, white, see white mutton curry*,
    142
  and prawn buriyani, see lamb
    buriyani*, 80
  with tomatoes, 143
Lentil(s) (dhal)
  about, 18
  dhal curry, traditional (parippu), 119
  moong dhal curry, 108
  moong guli, 203
  moong kavum, 202
  with spinach, see traditional dhal
    curry*, 119
  thatta vadai, 39
  purees in:
    prawn vadai, 154
    chana vadai, see prawn vadai*, 154
    idly, 87
    thosai, traditional, 85
    ulunthu vadai, 38
Liver(s)
  chicken, with onion and chili, 131
  curry, 140
Long beans
  about, 26
  with prawns and pepper, 155
Lotus root (nelum ala)
  about, 26
  badum, 113

M
Maldive Fish (umbalakada), about, 19
Mallum
  about, 19
  breadfruit, 56
  cabbage, 68
  coconut (also stringhopper sambol), 60
  kale, 71
  vara, 162
Mango
  curry (amba maaluwa), 109
  fantasy, 190

Marmite, about, 19
Menus, see authentic meals, 217-220
Measurements and suggestions, 31-32
Mild dishes, list of, 221-222
Murunga, see drumsticks
Mushroom
    badum (hathu badum), 122
    and fish pie, 164
Mutton
    curry, authentic, 141
    curry, white, 142
    rolls, 42

N
Nelum ala, see lotus root

O
Okra
    about, 26
    with anchovies and tamarind (nethali
        theeyel), 166
    theldala, 102
    see twice cooked fish*, 165
Onion(s)
    fried, and tomato sauce, fish in a, 170
    seeni sambol, 69
    seeni sambol buns, see fish buns*, 44
    see Pickles, Sinhala and Malay

P
Palm sugar, see jaggery
Pani pol
    about, 19
    bibikkan, 200
    crepes, honey-coconut, 187
    lavariya, 204
    naran kavum, 205
    stringhopper lavariya, see lavariya
Pappadam, about, 19
Pickle(s) (achcharu)
    about, 11
    jackfruit, tender, 103
    Malay, see Sinhala pickle*, 120

Pickle(s) (achcharu), continued
    Sinhala, 120
Pilau
    about, 19
    rice, 77
    stringhopper, 90
Pineapple
    fluff, 184
    sauté, spicy, 99
Plantain blossom badum (kessel muwa
    badum), 110
Plantains, see ash plantains
Polos, see jackfruit
Pork
    curry, traditional, 145
    kalu pol curry, 147
    in red curry, 146
Potato
    balls, 41
    curry, white, 117
    savory fried (ala theldala), 116
Prawn(s)
    Buriyani, lamb and, see lamb
        buriyani*, 80
    curry, piquant, 150
    with eggplant, 152
    with onion and chili, 151
    with pepper and long beans, 155
    sambol, 153
    vadai, 154
    wrapped in spicy pastry, 51
Pudding(s)
    avocado, 180
    caramel, 184
    mango fantasy, 190
    pineapple fluff, 186
    sago, 183
    wattalappam, 189
Pumpkin kalu pol curry, 112

R

Rice
  about, 20-21
  boiled, see steamed rice
  buriyani, lamb, 80
  buriyani, lamb and prawn, see lamb
    buriyani*, 80
  cilantro, 75
  fried, fragrant, 82
  milk (kiri bath), 74
  pilau, 77
  plain, see steamed rice
  steamed, 79
  tamarind (pulichatham), 78
  yellow, 76
Rhubarb,with custard sauce, stewed, 195

S

Sago
  about, 21
  pudding, 183
Salads, 53-71
  bitter gourd, crispy, 57
  breadfruit mallum, 56
  cabbage mallum,68
  carrot saladé, crunchy, 62
  coconut mallum, 60
  coconut sambol, 58
  cucumber saladé, cool, 67
  eggplant, traditional, 54
  egg, sassy, 64
  gotukola saladé, 63
  kale mallum, 71
  katta sambol, 66
  lunu miris, 65
  mackerel, 70
  mint sambol, 59
  seeni sambol, 69
  tomato sambol, 61
  vegetable rainbow, 55

Sambol
  coconut (pol sambol), 58
  katta, 66
  lunu miris, 65
  mint (minchi), 59
  prawn, 153
  seeni, 69
  stringhopper (co.onut mallum), 60
  tomato, 61
Semolina
  incorporated in:
    boroa, 212
    idly, 87
    payasum, 194
    uppu ma, 84
  steaming, 23
Sesame balls (thala guli), 208
Shrimp, see prawns
Spice(s)
  about, 21-23
  rack, Sri Lankan, 9
Snake gourd curry, see country cucumber
  curry', 104
Spinach with dhal, see traditional dhal
  curry*, 119
Squid
  curry, traditional, 176
  stuffed, serenade, 177
Staples
  coconut roti, savory (pol roti), 83
  godamba roti, 93
  godamba roti, egg, see godamba roti*,
    93
  hoppers, traditional, 91
  hoppers, egg, see traditional hoppers*, 91
  idly, 87
  koththu roti, 94
  pittu, 88
  stringhopper pilau, 90
  stringhoppers, 89
  thosai, traditional, 85
  uppu ma, 84
  also see Rice

Sugar candy, about, 23
Suggestions and measurements, 31-32
Sweeteners, exotic, about
  palm sugar (jaggery), 17
  treacle, 18
  sugar candy, 23
Sweetmeats
  aggala, 209
  aluva, 198
  athiraha, 199
  bibikkan, 200
  boroa, 212
  cookie, semolina and coconut, *see*
    boroa
  coconut toffee (pol toffee), 214
  jaggery milk toffee, 211
  kalu dodol, 201
  kokis, 206
  laddu, 213
  lavariya, 204
  milk toffee, jaggery, 211
  moong guli, 203
  moong kavum, 202
  naran kavum, 215
  stringhopper lavariya, *see lavariya*
  stringhopper asmi, 210
  thala guli, 208
  toffee, coconut, 214
  toffee, jaggery milk, 211

T

Tamarind
  about, 23
  anchovies with okra and (*nethali*
    theeyel), 166
  rice (*pulichatham*), 78
  twice cooked fish, 165
  also see gamboge
Thalana batu, see wild eggplant
Theldala, about, 23
Tomato(es)
  bitter gourd with, 105
  chicken with capsicums and, 127

Tomato(es), continued
  chicken with cilantro and, 130
  fish in a fried onion and, sauce, 170
  lamb with, 143
  sambol, 61
Treacle, *kithul*
  about, 18
  in desserts and sweetmeats:
    aggala, 209
    athiraha, 199
    avocado pudding*, 180
    bibikkan, 200
    moong guli, 203
    moong kavum, 202
    wood apple cream, 181
    banana fritters with, and coconut
      milk, 191
    also see pani pol

U

Utensils and apparatuses, 29

W

Wild eggplant (*thalana batu*), curry, 114
Wood apple
  about, 26
  cream (*divul kiri*), 181

V

Vegetable(s),
  about, 24-27
  salad, rainbow, 55
  sandwiches, 49
  see specific vegetables

Z

Zucchini, curry, *see* country cucumber
  curry', 104